# Color Planning for Interiors

## An Integrated Approach to Color in Designed Spaces

MARGARET PORTILLO, PhD

WILEY

Library of Congress Cataloging-in-Publication Data:
    Portillo, Margaret, 1962-
    Color planning for interiors: an integrated approach to designed spaces / Margaret Portillo.
        p. cm.
    Includes bibliographical references and index.
    ISBN 978-0-470-13542-6 (pbk.: alk. paper) 1. Color in interior decoration. I. Title.
    NK2115.5.C6P67 2009
    747'.94—dc22
2008021382

Printed in the United States of America

10  9  8  7  6  5  4  3  2  1

# Contents

Contents

# Acknowledgments

I most gratefully acknowledge the support of my colleagues and students from the Department of Interior Design at the University of Florida. First and foremost stands Siriporn Kobnithikulwong, who designed the illustrations for this book and always brought fresh enthusiasm and insights to our close collaboration. This book also has been enriched by the case contributors who, by sharing their scholarship and stories, deserve special mention: Justin Gunther, Laura Compton Busse, Tiffany Lang, and Julia Sexton. Other contributions to the developing project were made by Rozita Mozaffarian, Carly Jacobson, and James Wall.

I am especially appreciative of Joy H. Dohr, PhD, professor emerita of the University of Wisconsin–Madison, as well as the reviewers whose insightful comments on the manuscript helped shape the book. As a student under University of Wisconsin–Madison professor Marjorie Kreilick, my interest in color theory was ignited, and so too were the earliest seeds of the book.

I also thank Paul Drougas, editor at John Wiley & Sons, for believing in the potential of this project and offering his expert guidance in its development. I appreciate as well the fine contributions of Jacqueline Beach, senior production editor, and the diligent attention to quality color reproduction of the entire production and manufacturing team. Much thanks to Madeline Perri, copy editor extraordinaire.

I wish to acknowledge collectively the interior designers and architects whose projects greatly enrich this volume; they freely offer the readers of this book intimate access to their creative process, and this is truly inspirational.

I am most grateful to my husband, Norman Portillo, for offering his boundless encouragement throughout this adventure, and to our children, an energetic and colorful pair—Ellie Rose and Maxim.

# Introduction

This book is about color in interior design, and it explores several questions: What basic knowledge and applied research inform color planning? How do designers think about color, and what guides their processes? What lessons can be drawn from experienced designers, and how can this information guide future work? Over the years, the answers to these questions have fueled my teaching, research, and experience with color. They form the foundations of this book.

The book speaks to the depth and range of thought involved in designing with color. First and foremost, color must be considered in relation to context: form and light and materiality. Designers also employ color to communicate concepts or images in interior spaces as well as to engage the senses, affect decision making, and, to a certain extent, influence behavior. Further, color in inte-

riors may reflect designers' personal preferences or those of their clients or occupants of the space; other times, market trends, sustainability objectives, and material constraints influence interior coloration. It is my hope that awareness of the color functions framing this book—color as composition, associated meaning, human response, preference, and pragmatics—offers a way to expand the creative vision of designers.

Design innovation can be seen in this book's twenty original projects that illustrate color in design practice (see Table 1-1). These project narratives reveal multiple facets of color and offer a guide for thinking about color by demonstrating critical and creative thinking. In addition to process, the book emphasizes color research from anthropology, art, design, psychology, and marketing. Some chapters also include research notes that critique the methods, procedures, and findings of studies presented to help the reader become more discerning in evaluating strengths and limitations of applied color research. The need to leverage such studies in the design process is critical to the evolution of interior design as a field increasingly positioned as research-based. The application of research in design also figures prominently in current standards of the Council for Interior Design Accreditation.

## *Research Foundation of the Book*

When I began teaching color theory in an interior design program nearly twenty years ago, a research base on color decision making was practically nonexistent. Little, too, was known about key color qualities that designers think about, or about differences in the treatments of these qualities. To address this gap, I developed the Color Planning Framework from my research and have used its color criteria to organize this book.[1] Over one hundred color criteria, representing five distinct color functions, stem from this study, articulated by leading designers and colorists describing their projects in cities from San Francisco to New York. As a window into the design process, these criteria offer both structure and flexibility in developing color in designed spaces: a solid rationale for color planning and a bar for evaluation.[2, 3]

## *Organization of the Book*

*Color Planning for Interiors* comprises nine chapters on color theory, planning, and practice. Themes integrating color, lighting, materiality, and architectural form introduced in the first chapter continue throughout the book. To explicitly consider color processes, five obstacles to working with color that often go unexamined and unspoken are described in Chapter 1, which also presents the color planning framework of a contemporary residential project and a reexamination of color in Fallingwater. Chapter 2 presents classic theory and contemporary research on the art and science of color, describing constructions of color meaning, color systems, and color contrast theory. Chapter 3 introduces color perception, color testing, and color illusions that recognize the objective and subjective dimensions of color.

The core knowledge presented in the first three chapters segues into more detailed examination of the color criteria identified in the Color Planning Framework. Chapters 4–8 each address one color function. Chapter 4 examines color as a formal design element, while Chapter 5 centers on criteria for color preference research and color market cycles. Chapter 6 surveys the literature on color symbolism, emphasizing the role of color criteria in developing associative meaning such as

## NARRATIVES ON COLOR PLANNING IN DESIGN

**Chapter 1**

*Contemporary Color: Truth-to-Materials*

*Historic Color: Fallingwater*

**Chapter 4**

*Cinnabar: Residential Design*

*Firehouse Red: Adaptive Use*

*Kiwi and Tangerine: Workplace*

*Color Marketing: Model Condominium*

**Chapter 5**

*Integrated Color: Workplace*

*Kinetic Color: Workplace*

**Chapter 6**

*Corporate Color: Workplace*

*Regional Color: Three Resource Centers*

*Mid-century Modern Color: Workplace*

*Creative Color: Advertising Agency*

**Chapter 7**

*Understanding Color: Korean Luxury Shopping*

*Gourmet Color: Korean Speciality Market*

*Big-Box Color: Mexican Grocery*

*Calming Color: Spa*

*Healing Color: Neonatal Intensive Care Unit*

*Wellness Color: Pediatric Clinic*

**Chapter 8**

*Educational Color: K–8 School*

**Chapter 9**

*Experiential Color: Designing the Aquarium*

**Table 1-1**

Summary of project narratives by chapter

Introduction

brand identity. The human response to color is the topic of Chapter 7, which discusses the influence of color on arousal, emotion, cognition, and behavior in applied research and in workplaces, schools, and healthcare facilities. Chapter 8 focuses on practical considerations of color related to resources and materials, paying particular attention to color criteria for sustainable design.

Chapter 9 concludes the book by illustrating the way both additive and subtractive color systems create a memorable design experience in a world-class aquarium. The chapter also presents a first-person reflection on the experience of navigating a color-infused interior, revealing the reactions of a new visitor to an inspirational space.

**NOTES:**

1. Portillo, Integrating Color and Creative Vision: Color Criteria in the Design Process.
2. Portillo and Dohr, "Bridging Process and Structure through Color Criteria."
3. Portillo and Dohr, "A Study of Color Criteria used by Noted Designers."

# 1

# Color Planning Pathways

*Think of color as three-dimensional from the start. Color should provide clues as to what you are going to encounter in that environment. Color is the first thing you notice and the last thing you leave with.*

—Agnes Bourne, Interior Designer

Color elevates the human experience and transforms space; yet, the process of designing with color can be quite complex and challenging. When challenges to color planning are recast as opportunities for development, designing with color can be optimized and creativity unlocked. This book contains twenty narratives of design projects that reveal the ways designers use color to define form and create meaning while addressing human needs.

For experienced designers, color represents more than a name: red, yellow, or blue. *Hue,* or the family name of the color, simply represents its position on the visible spectrum, while the second dimension of color, *value,* indicates the relative lightness or darkness of the hue. Value defines the position of the hue in relation to black or white and the amount of light the color reflects. By gradually increasing the black in the color, less light is reflected, thus reducing its value. The opposite is true with white. Value can be gauged both achromatically and chromatically. *Chroma* is the third dimension of color. Also known as *intensity,* chroma defines the relative brightness or dullness of a hue; it represents the saturation level. Consciously considering dimensions of hue, value, and chroma gives designers more liberty to explore the potential of color.

Color planning does not stop with individual colors but necessarily extends to color groupings. Noted color theorist Josef Albers declared that color is the most relative element in art and astutely observed how some colors appear to shift in appearance when placed next to others. Color dimensions are relative to one another rather than absolute. A color that appears dark in one palette, for instance, may be judged lighter in another context, while a hue that appears bright in one palette may appear less saturated among other colors. In addition, color appearance is influenced by factors, such as lighting conditions and texture, that have implications for designing interiors. Color planning is much more than correctly anticipating how a swatch of color will translate an interior space.

The study of color is complex and can be understood in both subjective and objective terms. The subjective response to color is intuitive and varies from individual to individual. The objective response to color is rational and consistent, factual and standardized. Color research and knowledge, however, recognize both objective as well as subjective aspects of this design element. For example, the subjective naming of hues in a rainbow varies by culture, but its light wavelengths can be objectively measured in nanometers. The understanding of objective and subjective dimensions of color has been advanced in the following fields with particular relevance to the design of interiors:

- *Art:* Color interaction and contrast
- *Anthropology:* Cultural and historical color symbolism
- *Design:* Color planning narratives
- *Marketing:* Color and arousal, branding, and product differentiation
- *Physics:* Color and light properties and measurement
- *Psychology:* Color sensation, perception, and response

# Challenges of Color Planning

Designers face five challenges to color planning that, while potentially limiting, can be overcome through knowledge and experience (see Figure 1-1):

- *Subjectivity:* Color likes and dislikes
- *Objectivity:* Prescriptive color solutions
- *Conventionality:* Traditional schemes and harmonies
- *Materiality:* Natural coloration of materials
- *Dimensionality:* Visualization and application

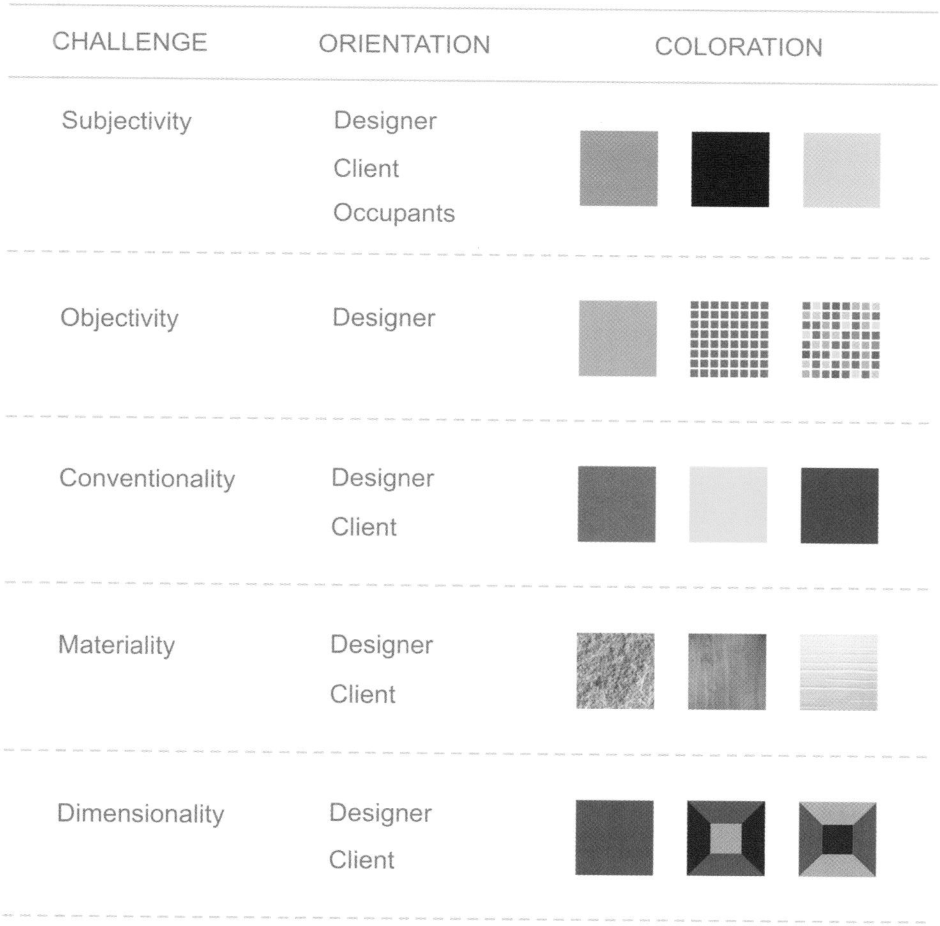

| CHALLENGE | ORIENTATION | COLORATION |
|---|---|---|
| Subjectivity | Designer Client Occupants | |
| Objectivity | Designer | |
| Conventionality | Designer Client | |
| Materiality | Designer Client | |
| Dimensionality | Designer Client | |

**Figure 1-1**

Challenges to color planning from designers, clients, and users with example colorations

## Subjectivity

Perhaps the most fundamental barrier to color planning is too heavy a reliance on personal preferences when designing. Research shows that humans prefer certain colors and tend to avoid others. As beginning designers reach beyond their subjective views of color, their confidence in working with myriad colors and materials grows as they align design intent with project context. Awareness of personal preferences and subjective beliefs about color may not even be conscious. This makes it important to reflect on the following questions: *What colors appear again and again in my own work and in the field? How can innovative and imaginative color palettes be introduced across market sectors?*

## Objectivity

If dangers arise from overemphasizing subjective beliefs, other barriers emerge from an overreliance on expert rules. For example, it was reported that a saturated pink, called Baker-Miller pink, subdued aggressive behavior in people being admitted into correctional facilities. Yet what was discovered over time was that prolonged exposure to this intense pink actually increased agitation. When a prescribed color formula is followed blindly, the result may not only lack imagination but also, however unintentionally, negatively affect human behavior.

The problem with one-size-fits-all recommendations is that they fail to account for context. Contextual considerations include the relationship between color and lighting, the influence of color on the amount of time to be spent in an interior, and individual differences in how color is perceived. Like inquiry on any topic, color research varies in quality and usefulness. To determine whether particular research findings should be applied to a design, begin by asking these questions: *Have the researchers carefully reported their methods, procedures, and participants? Have the color testing materials, lighting, and color vision of the participants been carefully controlled? In what types of settings can the findings be applied?*

## Conventionality

Another barrier to color planning is an overreliance on conventional color schemes. Traditional color harmonies surface in interior architecture with deadening regularity. While monochromatic, analogous, and complementary schemes, for instance, offer acceptable ways to organize color relationships, an unhealthy dependence on organizational rules blocks creativity. Traditional color schemes often focus on hue. However, all dimensions of color, including value and intensity, should be considered in relation to space and form. From a color planning perspective, conventional harmonies and schemes offer a beginning point rather than a solution. When developing color directions, consider the following questions to circumvent conventionality: *What is original and unique about the color palette? How is this coloration most appropriate for the design context?*

## Materiality

A further challenge is to recognize that materials and finishes, whether glass, granite, or paint, contribute color to interiors. Just as the hues of nature have inspired artists through the ages, introducing natural materials into designed spaces creates a coloration that is often nuanced and complex. Some designers and schools of thought embrace a truth-to-materials stance that celebrates materiality in design. This perspective elevates natural materials over applied color finishes, such as paint. Regardless of the design stance on authenticity, color planning should be approached with intention and purpose. This chapter presents a contemporary and historical narrative illustrating how interior color is created primarily with natural materials that unify and sculpt space as well as convey meaning. Rather than debating whether a painted wall is less authentic than a stone one or not fully considering the impact of materials selection on the overall palette, it is more critical to ask these questions: *Is the natural coloring of materials considered part of the color palette? How do material and finish coloration contribute to the architectural form and interior space?*

## Dimensionality

Another challenge is understanding color in three dimensions (see Figure 1-2). Developing color and materials palettes in two dimensions is not as complicated as applying these palettes to three-dimensional space. Sketch models, perspectives, elevations, and floor plans can facilitate visualization of color in the proposed design. Yet anticipating interaction of lighting and form on color placement, and viewing distance, scale, and proportion can be difficult even using the latest digital modeling techniques and physical mock-ups. One colorist I interviewed underscored the importance of careful and analytical observation: "Color expertise comes from experience. Look at color in the plane, where the color will be applied [on wall, ceiling, or floor surfaces], in the appropriate lighting at different times of the day. Consider the viewing distance when designing interior spaces." The coloration of materials can appear to change under different lighting conditions. To optimize the translation to three-dimensional color, consider these questions: *Has color been considered in relation*

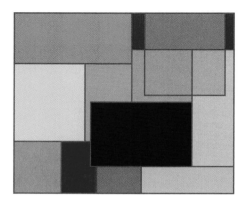
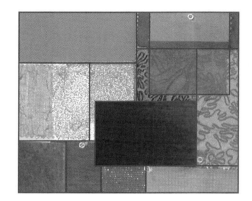

Color Planning for Interiors

*to form and space from the beginning of the design process? How can the visualization of color be developed through observation, experimentation with multiple media, sketch models, large samples, and mock-ups?*

# Color Planning Framework

The criteria-based framework presented in this book (see Figure 1-3) addresses five distinct functions of color and illustrates an integrated planning approach by specifically addressing:

- Color as *compositional element,* shaping space
- Color as *communication,* creating meaning
- Color as *preference,* reflecting individuality or market trends
- Color as *response,* arousing feelings and responses
- Color as *pragmatics,* responding to resource parameters

## *Color as Composition*

Working with color compositionally requires objective problem-solving to integrate color, lighting, and materiality. Individual colors also can be understood in compositional terms. For example, a white may be blue-based or red-based. Single colors can vary in the complexity of their composition. A neutral can be mixed from black and white (achromatic gray) or created from a pair of complements (chromatic gray). The complexity of color can be discovered by examining dimensions of hue, value, and chroma.

Further, groupings of colors can be analyzed compositionally. Establishing value relationships is particularly important for relating color to three-dimensional form. Color palettes offer a way to unify the interior with the exterior and can visually connect one interior space to another. Color also can create focal points and camouflage areas within an interior. Key concepts for color composition are complexity, balance, contrast, relationships, interaction, and integration.

## *Color as Communication*

Humans communicate with color and interpret color meanings. Color associations develop the conceptual design and enrich the more objective compositional approach to color. Professor Harold Linton explains, "Color must first convey an expressive meaning that is appropriate to the specific project for which a color solution is sought; and color and form must be presented to the observer in a manner that achieves visual unity."[1] Expressive color facilitates conceptual development and communicates both overt symbolism and subliminal connections that associate closely with the emotional aspect of color. Key concepts for color communication are identity, concept, ambiance, time, and place.

## Color as Preference

Color preferences influence the design process. Designers and clients have subjective color likes and dislikes that shape color planning. Further, individual preferences can be influenced by market trends and cycles where product offerings encourage the selections of current colors and finishes. Key concepts for color preference are signature color, personal identity, and market color.

## Color as Response

Color influences a range of human responses, from arousal to the ability to navigate complex buildings. The relationship between color and the human response is tangible but not fully understood or empirically established. Key concepts for the human color response include physiological, psychological, and behavioral responses, including spatial orientation and performance.

**Figure 1-3**
Color planning framework

8          Color Planning for Interiors

## Color as Pragmatics

Color in design also reflects practical realities. Resource constraints sometimes necessitate less expensive materials and finishes in given color ranges. Preconditions also may influence coloration. The logical starting point for developing a color palette is an existing material. For example, a precondition in an adaptive use project might be a prominent green terrazzo floor that must be retained. Maintenance issues affect the pragmatics of color as well. Designers typically select darker flooring for high-traffic corridors to extend the longevity of the specified material. In a related way, designing sustainably necessitates specific lighting levels, materials, and paint lines that influence color. Key concepts related to the pragmatics of color planning involve resources, preconditions, maintenance, and sustainability factors.

The following cases illustrate color planning concepts in two projects, one contemporary and one historic, that speak to the close relationship of color and materiality. The projects recognize the many considerations that enter color planning processes and the different levels of client involvement in the process.

# Contemporary Color: Truth-to-Materials

Larry Wilson, senior principal at Rink Design Partnership, Inc., described his process of designing with color in the Riverview condominium project (see Figures 1-4a, b). The primary source of this color palette was its materials: the expansive glass walls, quartersawn natural cherry, a 4-inch slab of natural Brecco DiVendome marble, black Galaxy granite, and Navona travertine. These materials played a defining role in creating the interior coloration of the 5,200-square-foot condominium.

The clients issued a straightforward objective: They wanted a contemporary space that was livable and conducive to entertaining, with a streamlined interior space that promoted ease of circulation while remaining secondary to the panoramic views of the waterfront. The building, located at the bend of a river, offered views in both directions; in Wilson's words, "There always was a show going on." The lighting from day to night dramatically changed the feeling of the interior space. Over the course of a day, lighting could shift from soft grays to clear blues to a light goldenrod and then culminate in a chromatic display at sunset; at night, glittering city lights illuminated the pitch-black sky.

Large glass walls fully exploited the view, and Wilson decided to treat the remaining walls in cherry. In addition to contributing to the formal shaping of the space,

*Left* **Figure 1-4a**
Interior with Brecco
DiVendome marble

*Right* **Figure 1-4b**
Interior with Galaxy
granite

color also reinforced the design concept by evoking the interior of a yacht; the clients were passionate about yachting (the firm also designed the interior of a 132-foot vessel for them). The designers carefully selected cherry as a primary material because it is close in coloration to teak, the traditional material for yachts, plus it allowed them to create the refined wall veneer in a way not possible with teak. The cherry veneer wraps the walls throughout the living room and dining areas and conceals continuous storage, a wet bar, and the mechanical utilities. Selected in part for pragmatic reasons, cherry created a warm palette for the interior, and its finish yielded a subtle reflected light.

Color contributed to a powerful interior architecture and elicited associations with water; however, color selections of materials and finishes also were pragmatic. Wilson recounted, "I chose the black Galaxy granite for several reasons. One of the difficult dynamics of work with residences on the river is that everything is constantly backlit from the strong sunlight. Maintenance becomes a big issue." The texture in the granite offers a highly functional surface with visual interest. He indicates, "I also chose the black Galaxy because it has an incredible copper metallic flex running through it. At night, under downlighting, it really comes to life."

Unique color and texture also surfaced from the selection of an imposing slab of Brecco DiVendome marble to create a custom bar requested by the clients. This focal point proved a challenge in terms of placement and functionality. The solution was to design a piece that could visually hold its own when not in use; the custom piece moonlights as sculpture, and its scale conveys a sense of presence without impeding the view.

The flooring selection also reflects pragmatic reasoning. Wilson states, "The floors are Navona travertine with a honed finish. It was chosen for its soft appearance and light reflectance. The combination of a light floor and light ceiling facilitated light bounce deep into the space. The honed finish eliminated glare and hid more soiling than a polished finish."

In summary, the color planning for the Riverview residence reflects intention and clarity. The color palette stems primarily from natural materials—glass, cherry, granite, marble, and travertine—yet the reasoning behind these selections addresses more than the inherent beauty of the materials. To create a fully integrated solution, the designer interwove compositional emphasis, symbolic meaning, and pragmatic reality, binding color to form. Wilson concludes, "I must say that form was the first consideration because it was driven by the programming information and functionality issues. Once the form was developed, the materiality and coloration were selected to reinforce the form."

# Historic Color: Fallingwater

*The "grammar" of the house is its manifest articulation of all its parts—the "speech" it uses. . . .When the chosen grammar is finally adopted (you go almost indefinitely with it into everything you do) walls, ceilings, furniture, etc., become inspired by it. Everything has a related articulation to the whole and all belongs together because all together are speaking the same language.*

—Frank Lloyd Wright, *The Natural House*[2]

Designed by Frank Lloyd Wright in 1936, Fallingwater embodies a unity of interior and exterior, architecture and building site, in one of the most architecturally recognizable residences in the world. Projecting over a waterfall in Mill Run, Pennsylvania, Fallingwater appears as one with the land, emerging from its surroundings. Inside, Wright deconstructed the box by challenging conventional precepts governing interior spaces with his design of an open plan that visually connects natural and built environments (see Figure 1-5a).

For the interiors, Wright selected the coloration and materiality with great precision. Local sandstone figures prominently in the primary living spaces and visually relates to the site, as does the rugged waxed stone floor. Besides natural stone, Wright specified only two paint colors for the interior of Fallingwater: light ocher and tonal

red. The ocher was inspired by the yellowing leaves of the rhododendrons on the site. Applied to both exterior and interior concrete, this paint coating creates a more neutral backdrop than would a saturated hue inspired by nature.

The second specified hue, Cherokee red, appears exclusively in a gloss finish on all metalwork at Fallingwater (see Figure 1-5b). The surrounding verdant landscape seems to intensify during the late spring and summer when viewed through Cherokee red window mullions. Wright favored Cherokee red and specified what became known as his signature color in brick, metal framework, flooring materials, and furniture in other commissions throughout his career. He even opted to have some of his automobiles painted in this hue. Why did he limit its application to the metalwork window and door frames in Fallingwater? Some scholars theorize that he associated Cherokee red with fire forming steel and iron; thus, he applied this color to metal surfaces only.

Documentation indicates that for Fallingwater, Wright's color planning process was both fluid and collaborative. It is not well known that his initial proposed coloration for Fallingwater was gold leaf, not light ocher. The change in thinking about the gold-leaf exterior stemmed from practical realities and client objections. The client, Edgar Kaufmann Sr., and his family also influenced the interior coloration. A department store magnate, Kaufmann was well educated, well traveled, and keenly

interested in design. As clients and creative partners, Kaufmann and his family introduced art, artifacts, and textiles into the space that shaped the interior coloration. All three members of the immediate Kaufmann family (Edgar Sr., Liliane, and Edgar Jr.) contributed to the design of the house, making recommendations to Wright that were incorporated into the final design. After the house was built, Liliane was integrally involved in decorating the interior spaces.

Fallingwater was meant to evolve and change over time, reflecting those who occupied the retreat. While the wall color of the interior architecture has remained the same, new objects and textiles have been introduced into the space over the years, contributing to a developing interior narrative. Edgar Kaufmann Jr. states, "Numerous decades and cultures enliven Fallingwater with art and artifacts, and neither these supplements nor the house and its setting were meant to remain static—Fallingwater grew and still grows."[3]

For example, the textiles covering the furniture have been changed numerous times since the original monk's cloth was selected by Wright. In its most recent reincarnation, Doria, a Jack Lenor Larsen fabric, covers the Wright-designed furniture and introduces a textured wool weave of red, yellow, and warm white into the space.

The following material detailing the interior color and material inspirations and origins of Fallingwater was written for this book by Justin Gunther, curator of Fallingwater.

## Red

Red, Wright's favorite color, was symbolic. He quoted Kliment Arkadevich Timiriazev, plant physiologist and author of *The Life of the Plant,* in the January 1938 issue of *Architectural Forum.* "The color red is invincible. It is the color not only of blood—it is the color of creation. It is the only life-giving color in nature, filling the sprouting plant with life and giving warmth to everything in creation."[4] In writing about his early years in Adler & Sullivan's offices, Wright recalled how the "red glare of the Bessemer Steel converters to the south of Chicago thrilled me as the pages of the *Arabian Nights* used to do—with a sense of terror and romance."[5] Frank Lloyd Wright scholar Donald Hoffmann contends that Wright's notion of Cherokee red may have been inspired by the soil color of what was once Native American territory in the Midwest.

Wright specified Duco paint, manufactured by the DuPont Company of Wilmington, Delaware, for the metalwork at Fallingwater. He asked DuPont to mix the paint to a "Cherokee red," sending along a Native American pot as a color guide.

As Hoffmann writes, "He used a product of modern technology to convey historic and even primal associations: red in homage to the Indian, red as an earth-color and symbol of the lifeforce, and, as Edgar Kaufmann Jr. remarked, red as the sign of fire in the working of metals."[6]

## Ocher

Wright originally wanted to surface the concrete of Fallingwater in gold leaf. Despite his love of red, Wright often praised gold, saying that "yellow is the color of creation, of the earth, of life, of death; gold is the highest life and blessedness after it."[7] He thought the moisture of the waterfall would transform the gold leaf with a rich and soft patina. Kaufmann, however, felt gold leaf was too extravagant and inappropriate for a mountain retreat. Wright then suggested a mica-white finish from Super Concrete Emulsions Ltd., a Los Angeles company. Kaufmann rejected this as well, saying the finish should blend with the stonework. Wright sent a sample in what he called the key "of the sere leaves of the rhododendron," inspired by the fallen leaves of the plant. As Hoffmann points out, "He had stained the outer walls of his Hollyhock House, on Olive Hill, to a light gray-green meant to echo the subtle hint of the olive leaves."[8] Cemelith, a waterproof cement paint from Super Concrete Emulsions, was chosen in August 1937. The order came to 1,340 pounds, and Kaufmann described the color as a light ocher.

> Color was very important to conveying Frank Lloyd Wright's aesthetic of organic architecture as a unified whole. He drew from two sources in determining his palette for a given project: the nature of the site and the nature of the building materials. In the early projects, particularly the Prairie houses that were constructed of brick and stucco, autumnal colors predominate: warm shades of red, gold, brown and yellow-green. These restful yet intense colors were accented by a palette of related hues and created a harmonious, unified and serene environment for the client. At Fallingwater, Wright employed both a limited palette of color and a limited number of materials in his desire to create an organic and integrated whole.
>
> —Lynda Waggoner, vice president and director, Fallingwater

## Black Walnut

Woodwork in black walnut was made by the Gillen Woodwork Corporation of Milwaukee in ship's quality to resist warping from the moisture of the falls. Although

Kaufmann believed the black walnut woodwork would darken the rooms, Wright and his on-site apprentices assured him it would provide a striking contrast between the furnishings, which are proportioned lower than usual, and the lighter gray stone walls beside and above them. In addition, contrasts in the wood itself add interest and reinforce the lines of the house. While many might consider the appearance of sapwood a flaw in the application of veneers, Wright chose to use the lighter lines of sap as a design element, bookmatching the flitches to create stunning highlights on cabinets, doors, and tables. Apprentice Bob Mosher reported to Wright that "E.J. [Edgar Kaufmann] thinks that walnut [is] too dark." But Mosher rebutted, saying "that a lighter wood would make everything too neutral in color, and that the contrast between the wood and stone would tend to make the stone appear lighter."[9] Wright loved wood as "the most humanly intimate of all materials," and he accepted veneers as a way of achieving continuity, of maintaining "the same flower of the grain over entire series or groups."[10]

### Wright–designed Furniture

Wright believed interior design should be integral to its environment. He designed the built-in furniture as well as a number of freestanding pieces for use in Fallingwater. The continuity of patterns in design from the structure and throughout the interior, carried along multiple scales, creates a rhythm, a harmony, and thus an environment of serenity and repose. Wright looked to nature as his guide in design, often intuitively understanding its lessons. Concepts such as the interrelation of part and whole and the importance of unifying structure and ornament are expressed from the original conceptual framework down to the smallest details. Four primary design motifs carried throughout Fallingwater and its furnishings are the horizontal line—the earth line, as Wright often referred to it; the cantilever—expressing freedom and expansiveness; the cascade—echoing the waterfall; and the semicircle—the soft curve of transition and balance. The furnishings maintain direct proportion with one another and with the building, which is proportionate to the site.

In Edgar Kaufmann Jr.'s words, Fallingwater's "free-floating seats," both the zabutons and the hassocks, help "to loosen everything up so it didn't look stiff. . . .[T]here are two sizes, the higher ones and lower ones. . . .It depends entirely on how laid-back you are, which ones you use."[11] By using seating of varying heights as well as seating proportioned lower to the ground than furnishings in more formal settings, Wright created a casual environment for the weekend home, one in accord with and conducive to people's natural patterns of gathering and conversation.

The lower seats, called *zabutons,* are essentially floor cushions and are found in the living room of both the Main House and the Guest House. At Edgar Kaufmann Jr.'s suggestion, they were made of latex foam—one of the first times the material was used in a residential setting. Surrounded by a walnut veneer frame, the cushions have a low, square shape and beveled sides. Upholstered with a red or yellow, heavily textured, wool blend Jack Lenor Larsen fabric called Doria, the zabutons create bright splashes of color against the grays and beiges around them. These small but highly visible bits of color act as "signposts of space." According to Edgar Jr., "They allow the eye to measure distances and areas by providing reference points. This is color used not only for decoration, but to organize space and structure intelligibly."[12]

To review, Riverview and Fallingwater illustrate color planning criteria in a truth-to-materials approach. Color relates structure to site and references nature with a limited materials palette. Color stories reference water and site characteristics as well as client self-expression and designer signatures. Both processes emphasize composition and symbolism; the Riverside narrative places more emphasis on color related to performance standards contributing to a functioning space, while the Fallingwater account speaks to client involvement in color decision making.

# Summary

The mastery of color can easily consume a lifetime of study. Students are well advised to learn from color in nature or in the city. Observation, experimentation, reflection, study, research, and practice work together to develop expertise in color.

This chapter discussed five challenges to color planning, beginning with an overemphasis on personal color preferences. A second limitation arises from a prescriptive approach to color. Another obstacle to color planning is an overreliance on conventional color schemes that not do fully consider color dimensions or context. None of the project narratives contained in this book conform to preordained color schemes but rather recognize multiple color criteria. The fourth challenge to color planning is the failure to consider specified materials as contributing color to interior spaces. The final barrier focuses on the difficulty of visualizing color three-dimensionally, which threatens the integration of color into the interior.

One way to gain a deeper understanding of color decisions in the design process is through project narratives. This chapter presented processes of designing color in a contemporary and a historic project. The color planning process evidenced in the Riverview condominium project resulted in a design that works spatially, emotionally, and pragmatically. The process behind the design of Fallingwater led to an integration of color, materiality, form, and site that transcends spatial conformity. Such narratives show commonalities and uniqueness in color planning pathways. To develop color relationships beyond the obvious, consider color in relation to form early in the design process and apply multiple color planning criteria to optimize the quality of interior spaces.

## NOTES

1. Linton and Rochon, *Color Model Environments*, 108.
2. Wright, *The Natural House*, 181.
3. Kaufmann Jr., *Fallingwater*, 96.
4. Wright, *Architectural Forum*, 102.
5. Wright, *Architectural Record*, 350.
6. Hoffmann, *Frank Lloyd Wright's Fallingwater*, 64.
7. Beyer, Eric Mendelsohn, 72.
8. Hoffmann, 61.
9. Mosher, Bob, letter to Frank Lloyd Wright, Fallingwater Archives, dated March 27, 1937.
10. Wright, *Architectural Record*, 481, 485.
11. Kaufmann Jr., edited text of Fallingwater discussion, Fallingwater Archives, dated May 31, 1974.
12. Ibid.

# 2

# Art and Science of Color

*Every objective color stimulus that we record from the outer world*
*corresponds with a subjective reaction from our inner world. The human*
*experience and response to color is as diverse as people themselves.*

—Gerhard Meerwein, Bettina Rodeck, and Frank Mahnke

Color vision develops as visual acuity sharpens during the first six months after birth. Infants see black and white before perceiving shades of gray. Researchers have demonstrated that even at two weeks of age, infants recognize the difference between red and green; however, the ability to distinguish more closely related colors does not develop for many months. This maturation occurs in a predictable sequence, as does cognitive development related to color identification and categorization. Some scholars believe the development of basic color terminology advances uniformly across cultures.

Classic research by anthropologists Brent Berlin and Paul Kay proposed that color words enter languages around the world sequentially, as illustrated in Figure 2-1. [1]

19

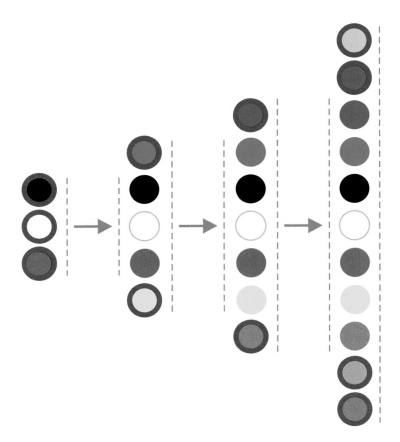

**Figure 2-1**
Berlin and Kay,
evolution of basic
color descriptors

In the least developed languages, people describe their world in black and white or light and dark (Stage I). At the next level, cultures add red to black and white (Stage II). Subsequently, green or yellow is introduced to enrich the terminology of black, white, and red (Stage III). This is followed by the addition of green and yellow to black, white, and red (Stage IV). More advanced cultures then add blue to black, white, red, yellow, and green (Stage V). Subsequently, brown expands the vocabulary of black, white, red, yellow, and green (Stage VI). Finally, languages with eight or more color descriptors include purple, pink, orange, and gray in addition to black, white, red, yellow, and green (Stage VII); the English language includes eleven basic color terms.

Berlin and Kay present this developmental pattern as cumulative and universal. While their research has generated some criticism, its widely accepted findings underscore the subjective nature of color. Although physical properties of color can be objectively measured, humans experience and express color differently based on culture, language, and experience. When asked to draw the sun, for example, children in the United States, without hesitation, color it yellow, while children in many Asian countries typically color the sun red or orange. Further, English, for instance, contains terms for blue and green, but the comparable Korean translation refers to *either* blue or green. This raises the question: Does a person who grew up speaking English *see* blue and green differently than native-speaking Koreans? Maybe. Color is not just out there in the environment; rather, humans actively construct the experience of color and are influenced by their cultures.

Communicating color meaning can be challenging. One of my interior design graduate students who had been an anthropology major commented to me how constrained he felt speaking Swahili because the language contains only one word signifying the color red. Just as he became frustrated at not being able to articulate color variations in this language, many beginning designers express similar exasperation at not being able to describe color precisely. This concern is justifiable, given the sheer number of perceptible colors. Scientists estimate that normally sighted people see up to 10 million hues. The English language contains approximately 1 million words and only eleven basic color terms. Thus, the colors humans are able to see greatly outnumber the words they typically use to describe their color perception. Other systems of organizing color are based on numbers, not words.

This chapter presents color systems and notations used to classify the wide array of hues seen. Each color system has a unique purpose that is discussed relative to its applications. The additive and subtractive color systems are first presented and compared; next, the Munsell system is overviewed and applied to a historic preservation case. The CMYK and RGB color printing and imaging systems are discussed, followed by an interior design project whose concept was inspired by these systems. The Pantone system is then introduced and applied to industry examples. Finally, a review of the artists' circle and its harmonies is extended to seven contrast principles illustrated in commercial and residential interiors.

# Color Concepts and Systems

## *Additive Mixing*
Additive primaries describe color mixing with light, while subtractive primaries are based on colorants and reflected light. Additive mixing occurs in light-producing

media such as televisions and computer monitors. Figure 2-2a illustrates additive primary and secondary colors. Primaries of red, blue, and green create the following secondary hues:

red + blue = magenta
red + green = yellow
green + blue = cyan

When combined, the additive primaries create white light, reflecting all wavelengths. Further, each combination of light produces a lighter mixture. The amount of the primary color introduced into the mixture influences the outcome. For example, a combination of red and green in varying proportions produces yellow, orange, or brown.

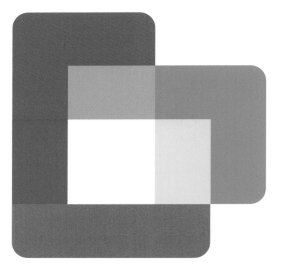

**Figure 2-2a**
Additive color (light)

## Subtractive Mixing

Subtractive mixing occurs in pigments, dyes, and printing processes that create color in paintings, textiles, or printed output. Subtractive primaries theoretically mix to black, absorbing all wavelengths. Each combination of colorants becomes darker. Figure 2-2b illustrates the subtractive primaries and secondary colors for pigments. Another subtractive system, CMYK, contains different primary and secondary colors:

Color Planning for Interiors

yellow + cyan = green
yellow + magenta = red
magenta + cyan = blue

The subtractive mixing of the CMYK system is expressed in the color illustrations and photographs in this book. Under ideal circumstances, the primary colors in pigments and paints produce black, but in practice, the resulting color often appears brown because of the quality of the pigment or density of the application. To counteract this effect, black is introduced as a fourth pigment to produce detail in color printing. The subtractive mixing of the RYB artists' circle is reviewed later in this chapter.

**Figure 2-2b**
Subtractive color
(pigment)

## *Munsell Color System*

Artist and teacher Albert Munsell proposed a color system for standardizing color measurement and communication. His opus, *A Color Notation,* conceptualizes color three-dimensionally, as shown in Figure 2-3a. While this internationally accepted system has been revised since its inception in 1905, it remains widely used today.

Derived from the empirical testing of human subjects, the Munsell system contains visually equal intervals of hue, value, and chroma. Color planes extending from the core of the model represent the principal hues of the system. The values for each hue extend vertically, while the chroma range for each hue reaches horizontally. Figure 2-3b illustrates the intervals of value and chroma in one hue.

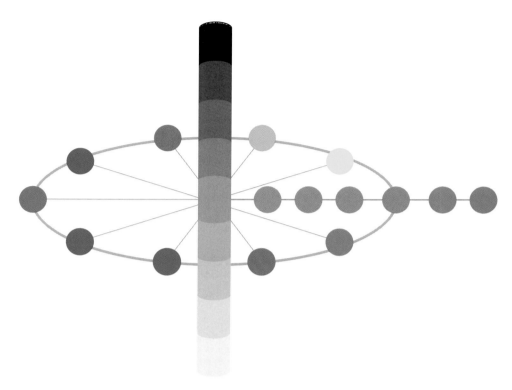

**Figure 2-3a**
Munsell diagram
illustrating hue, value,
and chroma

The original model contained ten visually equidistant hues circling the axis. The value dimension ranges from black (0) to white (10), with equally gray intervals positioned between the endpoints. Chroma is defined from gray (0) at the core of the model and extends to the physical properties of the color stimuli. Some highly saturated hues exceed chroma levels of 20.

The Munsell system contains five principal colors—red, yellow, green, blue, and purple—and five intermediate hues—red-yellow, green-yellow, blue-green, purple-blue, and red-purple—as shown in Figure 2-3c. Each hue can be divided into ten perceptually equivalent steps, ultimately defining one hundred hues. *The Munsell Book of Color* contains about 1,600 physical color chips representing the gamut of paint. A *gamut* is defined as the color range for a given medium, such as paint, color toner, or dye. The Munsell system can, however, be extended infinitely to describe any conceivable color in numeric terms.

For each color, the system assigns a representative notation—HV/C—indicating hue, value, and chroma. Language does not allow for precision color description,

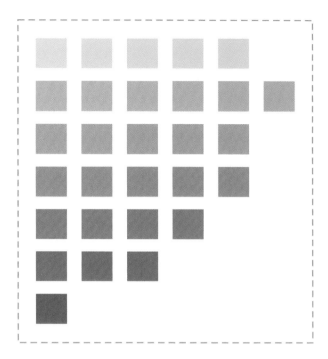

**Figure 2-3b**
Example of Munsell
green-yellow with
value and chroma
gradations

but the Munsell system does. Reds differ from one another; using Munsell, we can gauge that one red sample is 5R5/8 and another is 5R3/4. The reds are in the same hue range, but the first sample is lighter (5 versus 3 value) and brighter (8 versus 4 chroma) than the second.

This system defines the terms *tint, shade,* and *tone* in relation to value and chroma. The value of a hue can be adjusted to create a tint or a shade. Adding white to a hue creates a tint, a light value of the hue. A tint of red is pink. Mixing black into a hue creates a shade, a dark value of the hue. A red shade is commonly called burgundy. Tint and shade relate to value, while tone corresponds to the chroma dimension of color. A tone is defined as a hue with the addition of gray, dulling the saturation level. A tone of red is mauve. Another way to desaturate a hue is by mixing its complement into the base hue. Red can be toned with a small amount of green (its complement). Therefore, a tone can be created either by introducing gray or the complement into the base color.

While both strategies effectively lessen saturation levels, colors created by complements are more complex than those produced by gray. Complex colorations appear to shift more readily in appearance under different lighting or environmental

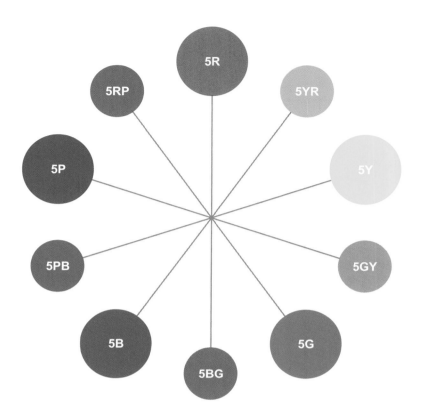

conditions. This phenomenon can be employed creatively by colorists and designers. Architectural colorist Donald Kaufman, for instance, creates full-spectrum interior paint colors that appear to change subtly in different lighting conditions. His techniques can be seen in numerous settings, including art museums and high-end residences. His approach is discussed in greater depth in Chapter 8.

Just as soil scientists accurately match samples of earth using the Munsell system, so do conservators conducting paint analyses in historic preservation work. For example, consultants relied on the Munsell system in restorations of landmark historic structures such as Wright's Fallingwater. The paint analysis of this property, completed in 1990, required a high degree of precision to ensure historical accuracy. Figure 2-4 contains the Munsell notation for the light ocher and Cherokee red paints specified for Fallingwater. The light ocher of the exterior and interior translates into Munsell notation 8.2YR7.2/3.7, with neighboring notations of 7.5YR7/4 (70 percent) and 10YR8/2 (30 percent). For the restoration, the light ocher paint

**Figure 2-4**
Munsell notation for
Fallingwater paint
color specifications

was specified in a matte finish. The Cherokee red translated into Munsell notation 8.3R3/5, with neighboring notations of 7.5YR3/4 (50 percent) and 10R3/6 (50 percent) specified in a gloss finish. After the color analysis was completed, these paint colors were custom-produced for the restoration.

## CMYK and RGB

Two systems make color printing (CMYK) and digital imaging (RGB) possible. The four-process CMYK (cyan, magenta, yellow, and black colorants) is an example of a subtractive system (see Figure 2-5). Mixtures of cyan, magenta, and yellow create a wide range of colors, while black (K) provides definition and contrast. In earlier times, black was known as the key color (or key printing plate) used to print detail in an image, typically with black ink. This subtractive system is used for inkjet and laser printing as well as for creating color images in magazines, newspapers, packaging, and the color imagery found in this book.

**Figure 2-5**
CMYK color system

RGB is an additive system where primary colors of red, green, and blue create white light (see Figure 2-6). The RGB system creates color in television and computer monitors. In digital design, predicting how color on the computer screen translates into colored output can be challenging. To minimize unwanted changes in coloration, computer programs are available to control conversions from RGB to CMYK.

**Figure 2-6**
RGB color system

Color! What a deep and mysterious language, the language of dreams.
— Paul Gauguin

**Figure 2-7**
Interior with wall
graphic

Interestingly, the CMYK and RGB systems inspired Gensler's design of Sun Chemical's headquarters. Given that Sun Chemical is the largest producer of inks and pigments across industries, the designers decided to relate the interior coloration of the workplace to the CMYK and RGB systems. Several murals feature abstract grids with these hues. Another large-scale mural celebrates the significance of color to the corporation with an inspirational quotation about its power (see Figure 2-7). Further, each of the office quadrants was assigned an accent color of cyan, magenta, yellow, or black to signify CMYK and the work group housed in it. More detailed information about this project is presented in Chapter 6.

## Pantone™ System

The company Pantone offers commercial color-specification guides for printing inks and other color-related services (see Figure 2-8). This company is noted for its Pantone Matching System (PMS), frequently used in the printing industry by graphic designers. The premise of PMS is that designers can color-match specific Pantone colors from the guides for exact re-creation across processes and media. These guides contain related groupings of printed colors, identified by name and number, and are available on gloss and matte paper.

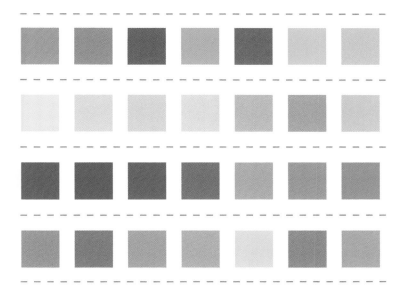

This system is also used for branding purposes when communicating a consistent and clear message is essential. For example, Sun Chemical's company logo is the Pantone color PMS 485C. Its reproduction on media as diverse as letterhead and wall graphics must adhere to PMS 485C. This ensures the red remains constant from application to application.

Pantone has combined pigments to yield colors not possible with the CMYK process. While CMYK is a four-color printing process, Pantone has developed a six-color process for producing a broader range of colors. This new process, however, requires special printing equipment. Finally, Pantone also sponsors proprietary marketing research on preferences of consumer groups and industry forecasting of color trends. This underscores the importance of color communication and marketing.

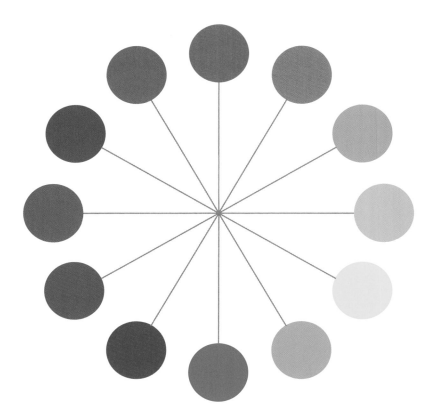

**Figure 2-9a**
Artists' circle
with twelve hues
(three primary, three
secondary, and six
intermediary)

## *Artists' Circle*

The artists' circle (also known as the *color wheel* or *artists' spectrum*) is an example of a subtractive system containing primary pigments of red, yellow, and blue. Theoretically, these hues mix to black; however, in practice, red, yellow, and blue mix to a neutral based on the amounts, composition, and purity of the pigments. As the result of reflecting light, pigments become darker every time they are mixed. Red and yellow always produce orange, but the orange varies depending on the amount and quality of the parent colors. Yellow mixed with blue creates green, while red combined with blue produces purple. Mixing primaries always yields the same hues; however, their quality varies with the relative amount of paint and pigment in the mixture.

Introduced at the earliest educational levels, the artists' circle offers a coherent way of organizing colors and can be used to teach paint mixing where yellow, red, and blue combine, in theory, to create secondary and intermediate hues. The quality

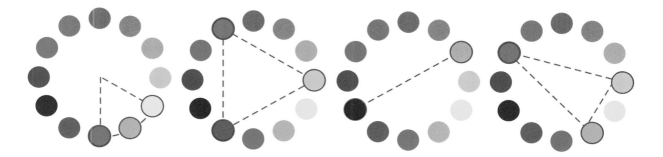

of these hues depends on the purity of the pigments. Figure 2-9a shows the resulting circle with three primary, three secondary, and six intermediate hues, while Figure 2-9b illustrates color schemes.

**Figure 2-9b**
Examples of color schemes (analogous, triadic, direct complement, split complement)

The color adjacencies on the circle indicate the degree to which the hues are related. For example, yellow, yellow-orange, orange, and red-orange each contain some yellow as a common denominator. The most strongly contrasting colors sit directly across from each other on the circle. When placed side by side, complements create contrast; however, when mixed, they neutralize the same blues that appear to have a greater contrast when thin lines separate the stripes on the right pattern.

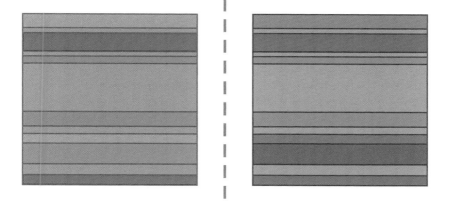

**Figure 2-10a**
Lower-contrast (left) and higher-contrast (right) palettes

## *Traditional Color Schemes*

The artists' circle is used to create color schemes based on principles of balance. A scheme characterized by strong contrast of hue is a primary triad creating a harmonic balance among yellow, blue, and red. These hues are equally spaced on the circle.

The secondary and tertiary triads offer less contrast than the primary triad because their colors have common denominators. For example, in the secondary triadic, yellow mixes into both orange and green, while red mixes into orange and purple; blue mixes into both green and purple. The same principle holds for triadic schemes with intermediate hues: yellow-green, red-orange, blue-purple and yellow-orange, red-violet, blue-green. All triadic harmonies are equally spaced on the circle.

Complementary schemes represent another high-contrast color harmony. The basic principle underlying complementary colors is that the hues are positioned opposite one another on the artists' circle. Placing them side by side accentuates their difference; mixing them creates a neutralized complementary gray. Simple (or direct) complementary schemes consist of two colors positioned directly across from one another on the circle. There are six complementary pairs. The first set of complements consists of a primary and a secondary color: yellow and purple; red and green; blue and orange. The remaining three complementary pairs consist of the following hues: yellow-green and red-violet; blue-green and red-orange; yellow-orange and blue-purple.

Direct complementary schemes contain two hues; split complementary schemes contain three colors. Split complements create a Y-shape on the circle. For example, yellow's companion colors are red-purple and blue-purple. Here, the twelve split complements are yellow, red-purple, blue-purple; yellow-orange, purple, blue; orange, blue-purple, blue-green; red-orange, blue, green; red, yellow-green, blue-green; red-purple, yellow, green; purple, yellow-orange, yellow green; blue-purple, yellow, orange; blue, yellow-orange, yellow-red; blue-green, orange, red; green, red-orange, red-purple; yellow-green, red, purple. Another

**Figure 2-10b**
Tonal manipulations (achromatic gray and chromatic grays with complementary pairs)

variation on the complementary scheme is the double complement scheme, with four hues.

Analogous schemes contain three or four neighboring hues on the color circle. For example, yellow could be included in the following analogous relationships: yellow, yellow-orange, red-orange; yellow, yellow-green, green; or yellow-green, yellow, yellow-orange. When yellow mixes into all the hues in this example, the resulting scheme contains less contrast than the triadic or complementary harmonies do.

Monochromatic schemes are defined by variations on a single hue. Subtle contrasts of tint, shade, and tone create unity with less contrast. While monochromatic schemes employ a single hue varying on value and chroma, achromatic schemes (without color) consist of variations of black, white, and gray.

Traditional color schemes are defined as triadic, complementary, analogous, monochromatic, and achromatic. While these schemes typically have been incorporated in interior design curricula, increasingly, color should be reconsidered with materials and lighting in an integrated context.

# From Art to Design: Itten's Contrasts

Insightful observations on the nature of color were formulated by theorist, painter, and Bauhaus instructor Johannes Itten. Over several decades, Itten developed ideas that culminated in the book *The Art of Color: The Subjective Experience and Objective Rationale of Color.* The abridged version of this book remains in print today and can be found on the syllabi of art and design courses in higher education. Itten created his own variation of the artists' circle, shown in Figure 2-11, but, more significantly, he enumerated seven types of color contrast found in two-dimensional applications. Being able to control the amount of contrast allows one to define focal points with color as well as to camouflage.

**Figure 2-11**
Itten's color star

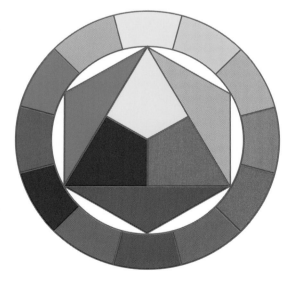

Exploratory research by Madeline Sattler examined the ramifications of Itten's contrast theory for interior design. The study found the most compelling quantitative evidence for temperature contrast defining twelve controlled interior settings.[2] She speculates that warm-cool contrast may be particularly useful in designing interiors to convey expressive and compositional aspects of color. According to Itten, warm colors associate with the sun, heat, and dryness, while cool colors signify shadows, coolness, and humidity. Compositionally warmer hues create a feeling of spatial compression, while cooler colors appear to expand interior space.

## Hue

Designers can employ color to create areas of emphasis within interiors; the greater the difference between hues, the greater the contrast. The more direct method simply involves creating contrast through hue. For instance, alternating orange and blue stripes create hue contrast. Obviously, if the lines were the same shade of blue or orange, there would be no contrast and no distinction. The green also creates hue contrast in the space, although at a lesser degree than the orange and blue. Contrast of hue, as well as the other six contrasts, illustrates the relativity of color.

Figure 2-12a shows hue contrast in variations of orange and blue, while Figure 2-12b illustrates hue contrast in a transition space. The intent was to create a stimulating common area in this workplace. The tonality, textural variation, and lighting pattern reflected on the ceiling plane help control the level of contrast.

**Figure 2-12a**
Contrast of hue
(orange-blue-green
interactions)

*Top* **Figure 2-12b**
Contrast of hue in
interior design

34 Color Planning for Interiors

## Temperature

Another way of classifying color is through temperature. Again, *color temperature* can refer to an objective, thermal quality that can be gauged, or the term may indicate the subjective, perceived warmth or coolness of a hue. The following example illustrates the intersection of objective and subjective perceptions of color; a room painted in what is defined as a cool color is perceived as 6–8°F cooler than one painted in a warm color. Even though the actual temperature in the room remains constant, people report feeling a significant change in perceived temperature based on the wall color.

According to Itten, the color circle can be evenly divided into warm colors (yellow, yellow-orange, orange, red-orange, red, red-purple) and cool colors (purple, blue-purple, blue, blue-green, green, yellow-green). Placing combinations of these hues side by side heightens the perceived level of temperature contrast. Context is critical, however, in gauging the apparent temperature of a hue. For example, green will appear warmer against a red background than against a yellow-green one. Figure 2-13a illustrates contrast between warm (orange/copper) and cool (blue/glass). The warm-cool contrast positions the central brushed copper oven as a focal point in the contemporary Italian restaurant shown in Figure 2-13b.

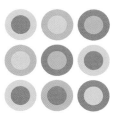

**Figure 2-13a**
Contrast of temperature (orange-blue interactions)

*Top* **Figure 2-13b**
Contrast of warm-cool in interior design

## *Value*

The contrast of light and dark is critical in three-dimensional design. According to Joy Luke Turner, past president of the Inter-Society Color Council, "The light and dark relationships between colors in a room, or among any other group of colors, create strong visual patterns: although they are usually not noticed by the public, whose attention is directed at hues rather than values."[3] Focusing on the dimension of value, artist Ad Reinhardt created a series of black canvases between 1951 and 1967. At first glance, the canvases appear to be black, solid, and undifferentiated; however, closer examination reveals faint hues buried in the black surfaces. The artist may be challenging the viewer's sensitivity to color within black and his ability to look beyond the surface.

Subjective meanings of dark or black colors extend from sophistication and opulence to evil and decay; objective measurements of values ranging from white to gray to black, considered "colorless hues," can be gauged in the Munsell system. Munsell notation for white is N/9.5/0, and the notation for black is N2/0, while a middle gray is N5/0. The N indicates these neutrals contain no hue; the zero signifies a lack of chroma. The dimension of value also describes the relative lightness or darkness in hues. A study of values illustrates this contrast in Figure 2-14a, while the restaurant interior in Figure 2-14b illustrates how the contrast of light and dark creates a sense of intimacy, reinforced by low lighting levels.

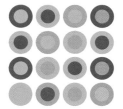

## *Saturation*

Some colors, by their nature, are more saturated than others (see Figure 2-15a). On the artists' circle, for instance, yellow (5Y8/11) is stronger in chroma and significantly lighter than purple (5P3/7). Sharing more similarities, a secondary orange (5YR6/11) is chromatically equal to the yellow but slightly darker in value. A highly saturated hue creates a focal point in many natural and built environments, while a desaturated hue deflects attention in more neutral settings. Note, however, that a brightly patterned animal or object can blend into a highly saturated environment (think of a butterfly in the rainforest); this is called *dazzle camouflage.* The contrast of saturation is at work in Figure 2-15b, where the yellow-based neutral of the column contrasts with the surrounding purples. However, the light-dark contrast creates even stronger emphasis within the room.

## Complements

Complementary colors offer another way to produce contrasts. Itten rightly observed that placing complementary colors side by side heightens their contrast. A blue appears more vivid next to an orange, while mixing blue and orange paint creates a chromatic neutral, known as a *complementary gray.* This mixture is more complex than an achromatic gray because it incorporates two complementary hues. Figure 2-16a illustrates a complementary scheme, and its companion, Figure 2-16b, shows a creative interpretation of this traditional color pairing in the design of a workplace. The highly contrasting blue and orange stripe works well in conjunction with the more tonal variations of these hues found in materials that offer not only color variation but also textural contrast.

**Figure 2-16a**
Contrast of complements (orange-blue interactions)

*Top* **Figure 2-16b**
Contrast of complements in interior design

## Simultaneous Contrast

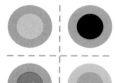

**Figure 2-17a**
Simultaneous contrast (red-black–tonal green)

*Top* **Figure 2-17b**
Simultaneous contrast in interior design

Simultaneous contrast creates an illusion wherein color appearance seems to change with the background color, typically in the direction of its complement. A red circle, for example, placed on a green field appears even more saturated in hue. Essentially, colors look differently depending on the surrounding context, as shown in Figure 2-17a. Simultaneous contrast also occurs with achromatic neutrals. A medium-value circle appears darker on a light background and lighter on a dark one. Anticipating the effects of simultaneous contrast helps prevent unwelcome surprises. This contrast principle underscores how colors exist in relation to one another and is particularly relevant in interior design, where the appearance of colors and materials can change significantly in context and juxtaposition. Figure 2-17b illustrates simultaneous contrast; the rose intensifies in hue against the tonal wall.

Color Planning for Interiors

## Extension

Like the contrast principles already discussed, contrast of extension emphasizes colors in relation to one another. Also known as *contrast of proportion,* this concept focuses on the relative amounts of colors used and is particularly relevant to the design of interior environments. (Chapter 4 presents a project that contains a lesson about this color contrast.) In actuality, hue choice can be of less concern than the amount and placement of the color within the interior. Figure 2-18a illustrates the contrast of extension two-dimensionally where the ratio of orange to gray varies. This contrast is shown in a cafeteria in Figure 2-18b, where the wall murals incorporate the same orange, white, and gray tiles in different amounts to great effect.

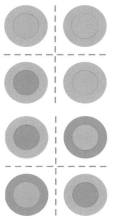

**Figure 2-18a**
Contrast of extension
(orange-neutrals)

*Top* **Figure 2-18b**
Contrast of extension
in wall mural

# Summary

This chapter describes the evolution of basic color terms across cultures, illustrating how humans actively construct the experience of color. Subjective color meaning coexists with objective systems of color classification, measurement, and specification, including Munsell, CMYK, RGB, and Pantone. Each system has its own applications, its advantages as well as limitations. The artists' circle is a time-honored method for creating color schemes. Color harmonies and preferences vary from individual to individual, time period to time period, and culture to culture, underscoring the subjective aspect of color. Integrating color with lighting and materials in interiors necessitates going beyond color harmonies. Finally, the chapter presents classic color theory on seven contrast principles defined by Itten that can foster new and original thinking about color in designed spaces.

## NOTES

1. Berlin and Kay, *Basic Color Terms.*
2. Sattler, *A Method for Analyzing Three-dimensional Color Interaction.*
3. Turner, *The Munsell Color System: A Language for Color,* 8.

# Color Perception

*In every second of observation, the interactions of light, surface, and human perception create hues anew. And because sensitivity to color differs among individuals, each person's perception will be unique in some way, based on what he has just perceived and all that he has perceived before.*

—Donald Kaufman and Taffy Dahl

Color and light are inextricably tied. Lighting influences color appearance, as do the physical qualities of the object being viewed. The eyes and brain form the visual system, which affects color perception. Color acuity also is affected by factors such as age and genetics. Thus, as shown in Figure 3-1, the ability to view and perceive color involves:

- light
- object
- visual system

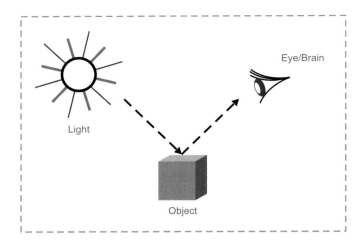

**Figure 3-1**
Color perception
engages light, object,
and visual system
(eye and brain)

# Color Constancy

*Color constancy* refers to a phenomenon where humans view the color of an object as remaining the same in spite of changes in lighting. For example, the principle of color constancy dictates that individuals will always see the yellow series of doors shown in Figure 3-2 as yellow, even though the hue neutralizes under lower lighting conditions. Color constancy is an adaptive mechanism that allows humans to perceive their environments as visually cohesive rather than confusing. From an early age, children generally describe shadows as black, snow as white, and trees as green, and over time forget to really see the distinctions within those colors. Yet it is possible to become more aware of variations in color and lighting and to build greater perceptual sensitivity. Looking for color nuances in shadows, snow, and foliage is one way to begin to see the world from a new perspective.

**Figure 3-2**
Color constancy

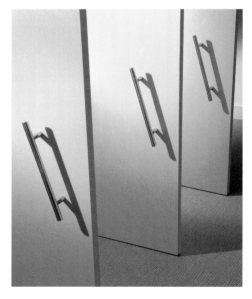

# Lighting Processes

Humans are able to see wavelengths of approximately 380 to 720 nanometers (nm). This visible interval is located on a small segment of the electromagnetic spectrum, shown in Figure 3-3. The visible spectrum contains red, orange, yellow, green, blue, indigo, and violet wavelengths, and it extends in lockstep progression from the shortest wavelengths (violet, 380 nm) to the longest wavelengths (red, 720 nm). All the colors of the spectrum together create white light. In nature, red wavelengths invariably form the overarching curve atop the rainbow. In the built environment, lighting containing red gels or filters emits the most powerful colored light as well.

Properties of lighting and illumination influence color appearance. From a broader perspective, the lighting design process shares similarities with color planning. A study by Tripti Kushwah documented the criteria employed by a noted lighting design firm in three San Francisco museum installations.[1] Her findings indicated that museum lighting criteria paralleled color criteria in terms of:

1. The way lighting shapes space *compositionally*
2. The ability of lighting to create overall *ambiance*
3. The influence of lighting on the *occupants* of the space
4. The lighting *preferences* of the designer and the clients
5. The *pragmatic* issues of lighting such as energy use and conservation

Early in the design process, the overall patterns of lighting can be explored. Figure 3-4 shows value studies of lighting in the preliminary stages of a restaurant design, where illumination and value influence form-making and ambiance. Figures 3-5a, b compare two conference rooms in which color and lighting affect the perceived scale and spirit of the spaces. One conference room is fairly neutral, with lower lighting that contributes to a feeling of spaciousness and calm (Figure 3-5a).

**Figure 3-3**

Visible segment of the electromagnetic spectrum

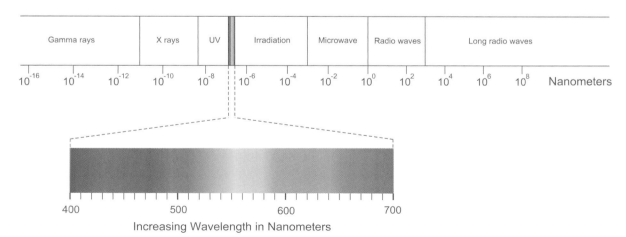

Increasing Wavelength in Nanometers

*Above* **Figure 3-4**
Achromatic studies
of lighting and value
relationships

*Below* **Figure 3-5a**
Neutral conference
space

*Opposite* **Figure 3-5b**
Chromatic conference
space

The other conference room has a saturated blue wall color that wraps onto the ceiling plane and contrasts with the circle of red Eames chairs (Figure 3-5b). Flooded with light, the ceiling appears to dissolve in this compressed interior, which exudes a vibrant and energetic quality.

Color theorists and design practitioners frequently argue that value—the inherent lightness or darkness of a color—should begin the color planning process. Understanding value relationships is essential because highlight and shadow define form and space, creating or contradicting three-dimensionality. Understanding this dimension elevates color beyond a surface treatment on the floor, walls, and ceiling. In his color consultancy, Kaufman advocates establishing the values first when developing color for interior architecture, before considering hue and chroma, because value relates directly to the underlying structure of the three-dimensional space. He also concentrates closely on the color placement within the space, so the color sequencing flows from room to room. Color should be considered carefully in relation to architectural breaks, which can be especially challenging in open-plan interiors.

The dimension of chroma also warrants particular attention. In an empirical research study, Patricia Raney examined color-mixing strategies in relation to creative problem-solving, specifically elaboration.[2] The color planning strategies of two groups of students were compared: those with stronger creative elaboration and those who were weaker in this form

*Left* **Figure 3-6a**
Warm color
temperature

*Right* **Figure 3-6b**
Cool color
temperature

*Pages 50–51*
*Left* **Figure 3-6c**
Hyatt Regency suite
with achromatic view
(Chicago)

*Right* **Figure 3-6d**
Hyatt Regency suite
with chromatic view

*Pages 52–53*
*Left* **Figure 3-6e**
Hyatt Regency warm
materials palette

*Right* **Figure 3-6f**
Hyatt Regency cool
materials palette

of creative thinking. The high elaborators mixed colors differently than did their less creative counterparts. Using only a complementary pair of hues with black and white, the creative thinkers not only produced more colors but also mixed greater tonal variations from the hues. Their approach differed significantly from the less creative students, who focused primarily on mixing hues and tints of those hues but rarely developed tones. This well-controlled study emphasizes the integral connection between creativity and a more nuanced understanding of color.

Designers have tremendous opportunities for creating color-light interaction, in which lighting temperature appears to shift color subtly or to great dramatic effect. Figures 3-6a, b illustrate a comparison of warm and cool lighting in the same stairwell of a corporate headquarters. In a hotel suite, the black and white photographs mounted on a gray wall feel cool in temperature (Figure 3-6c). From another angle, the painting creates a warmer feeling in the space (Figure 3-6d). Color and materials palettes likewise can appear warm (Figure 3-6e) or cool (Figure 3-6f). These are two options from a hospitality project. Changes in lighting temperature are expressed in the series of images in Figures 3-7a–c, which show a fairly theatrical application. The increasing possibilities for colored lighting applications in interiors are exciting. Also of interest are color effects and illusions, described in the remainder of this chapter.

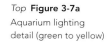

Top **Figure 3-7a**
Aquarium lighting
detail (green to yellow)

Bottom Left **Figure 3-7b**
Aquarium lighting
detail (yellow to orange)

Bottom Right **Figure 3-7c**
Aquarium lighting
detail (red to magenta)

*Color Perception*     49

## *Metamerism*

An illusion called *metamerism* occurs when an object color appears to change under different light sources. A metameric pair is two objects that seem identical in color under one light source but not under another. The phenomenon arises from differences in the spectral curves of the objects being compared. The illusion emphasizes the integral relationship of color to light to object, and it stems from differences in the physical makeup of colorants introduced into materials (e.g., paper, plastics, metals, and fabric) and their varied responses to light. Even two color prints using different CMYK inks appear to change under different light sources.

Industries trying to achieve color standardization and consistency in their products want to avoid metamerism at all costs. For example, automobile manufacturers want the interior components and materials in their cars to appear unified and consistent under both bright and dim lighting conditions; consumers do not want their well-coordinated car interior to look dirty or discolored under another lighting condition. For example, certain materials and finishes in a brown interior may appear a greenish khaki in the evening.

# Visual System

## *Color Perception*

Light wavelengths enter the eye through the cornea, pass through the pupil, and strike the fovea within the retina at the back of the inner eye. The wavelengths prompt an electrical-chemical reaction in the visual system by stimulating the millions of rods and cones in the retina. While the rods perceive contrasts in low light levels, the cones identify color through red, green, and blue cells. The cones sensitive to long wavelengths respond to red. Those that detect medium wavelengths react to green, and those sensitive to short ones respond to blue. When stimulated, these cells trigger signals to the visual cortex in the brain.

Color vision depends on the normal functioning of the visual system; however, selective damage to either the eye or the brain can result in impaired color vision. While an estimated 8 percent of men and 0.04 percent of women have some type of defective color vision, complete color blindness—that is, perceiving the world as achromatic—is exceedingly rare. The most common problem is the inability to distinguish reds and greens. People with this type of impairment see both red and green as brownish. Therefore, the term *color-blind,* as commonly used, is a misnomer.

## Color Vision Assessment

This section presents two standardized instruments for assessing color vision. Color plate measures, such as the Isihara Color Plate test, contain embedded figures used for testing color vision. Individuals with normal color vision can distinguish a recognizable image, such as a number within an overall pattern, whereas those with impaired color vision cannot see anything within the pattern. Plate tests offer an overall assessment of color vision; more specific measures of color acuity require another type of testing.

For example, the Farnsworth-Munsell (FM) 100-Hue test involves sorting a randomized series of nearly identical color chips into a correct order between two set endpoints. Under a full-spectrum light source, the test subject must sort four trays totaling eighty colored caps. The Munsell system was used to standardize these color progressions of minute variations in hue, value and chroma remaining constant. One tray, for example, requires sorting twenty-four nearly identical hues in order between a yellow-green and a green endpoint. Test performance is recorded as normal, superior, or deficient. Research on noted designers found that performance on the FM 100-Hue test was significantly higher than the norm, indicating these designers had greater color acuity than the general population. What is not known from these findings, however, is if the designers were born with this characteristic or whether occupational training increased their color acuity over time. A combination of both factors is the probable explanation.

Professor of fine arts photography Richard Zakia recognizes that in his field certain tasks require color acuity: "If a computer monitor is being used by more than

Left **Figure 3-8a**
Tonal limited palette

Right **Figure 3-8b**
Monochromatic
limited palette

one person, and one of the users has a color deficiency, such as a reduced sensitivity to a particular hue, this may cause a problem. It is particularly important that subjects selected for critical color judgment tests be tested for any color deficiencies. It is important for judges of color photographic contests to have normal color vision."[3]

Not only photographers but also practitioners ranging from gemologists to textile scientists require superior color acuity. Certain occupations require color vision screening of potential employees, and those in design fields also may be interested in gauging color vision. Like other natural physical aptitudes, the ability to perceive color is an innate trait that can be developed through education and experience. One way to do this is to explore color mixing across media, focusing on certain dimensions of color, such as producing a systematic progression of tones within a single hue. The color study in Figure 3-8a illustrates a limited or neutral palette, while Figure 3-8b shows a range of possible variations in greens that vary in terms of temperature, value, and intensity.

## Successive Contrast

Successive contrast occurs when the perception of a new color appears after exposure to another color, creating what is referred to as an *afterimage* or *ghost color*. For example, if an individual stares at a saturated red circle without blinking and then looks at a white surface, she will see a pale green afterimage. Successive contrast explains how humans see colors that are not physically present.

Several examples illustrate practical applications of successive contrast. Surgical staff members develop afterimage problems and eye fatigue after looking at exposed tissue for long periods. They therefore wear green scrubs to help prevent "seeing spots." Likewise, to combat eyestrain when designing, architectural drafting tables traditionally were covered with a light tonal green material.

## Simultaneous Contrast

Simultaneous contrast occurs when the color of hues placed side by side appears to change (see Figure 3-9). This phenomenon fascinated professor and painter Josef Albers, who studied the effects of simultaneous contrast for many years. His lifelong interest in color began at the German Bauhaus school of design and continued during his tenure at Black Mountain College and Yale University, where he directed hundreds of students in the systematic exploration of color. Recognizing color's ability to change across contexts, Albers and his students demonstrated color illusions in a series of non-objective, two-dimensional studies using silk-screened paper. For

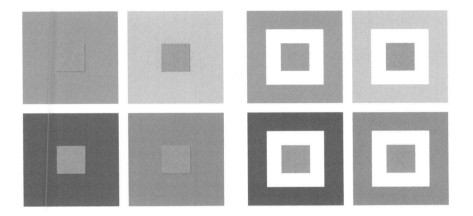

example, one illusion demonstrated how one color could look like two radically different hues; another illusion showed the background field color could make two very different hues appear the same. The resulting portfolio of these studies was aptly titled *The Interaction of Color,* and an expanded edition of this classic text was reissued in 2006. Albers showed that neutralized color offers the greatest potential for shifts in appearance. Chromatic neutrals can be particularly chameleonlike, changing dramatically with different color adjacencies and lighting variations.

## *Transparency Effect*

The illusion of transparency was another effect Albers explored. This illusion creates a feeling of spatial depth in two-dimensional applications by overlapping shapes. A straightforward example shows green where a band of blue intersects a band of yel-

low. In addition to manipulating space compositionally, this illusion creates a sense of mystery by revealing and concealing information. In designed spaces, transparent panels of frosted glass, for example, create a sense of openness and light while screening more private spaces. The transparency illusion can be demonstrated using paint, colored paper, or digital media. All three dimensions of color—hue, value, and chroma—must be carefully controlled to create a convincing illusion. Figure 3-10a illustrates how the color of the transparency is clearly positioned between its parent colors.

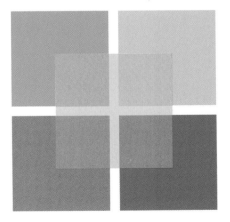

Transparencies created in art are illusory; transparencies in design involve materiality and space. Figures 3-10b–d show three conferencing areas in an advertising agency. Maintaining privacy in

Top **Figure 3-10b**
Transparency in interiors

Bottom **Figure 3-10c**
Transparency in interiors

Opposite
**Figure 3-10d**
Transparency in interiors

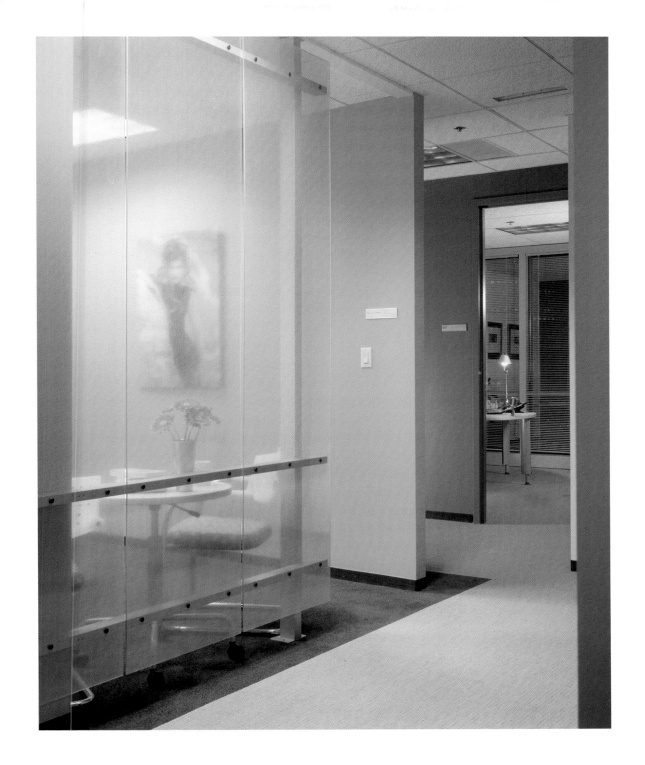

an open office plan can be addressed with glass manufactured to different gradations of transparency. Further, transparencies allow for a continuity of color within interior spaces. Again, the inherent transparency of treated glass panels allows for visual access and signals open communication but also affords people meeting within the conference areas to remain focused and productive.

## *Optical Mixing*

Optical mixing occurs when humans visually mix or fuse colors into a unified whole. Design applications of optical mixing include mosaics, murals, and textiles. The scale and patterning within the design of the tiles, paint strokes, or fibers influence color fusion, as does viewing distance. Optical mixing typically results in a richer coloration that would not be possible from a single color. The graphics in Figures 3-11a, b illustrate optical mixing using three hues and two hues, respectively. From a functionality standpoint, optical mixing in carpet fibers and textile patterns contributes to durability and longevity.

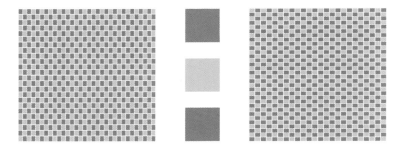

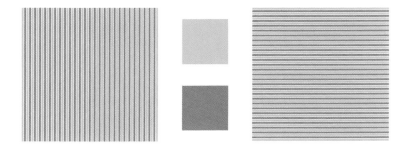

*Top* **Figure 3-11a**
Optical mixing with
primary triad

*Bottom* **Figure 3-11b**
Optical mixing with
greater fusion using
horizontal rather than
vertical lines

## Bezold Effect

The Bezold effect, also referred to as *assimilation,* is an illusion in which the overall value key of a pattern seems to change. Specifically, when patterns incorporate a repeating white element, the whole pattern appears lighter; conversely, when the pattern includes a repeating black element, it looks darker. Viewed as a whole, the pattern or design appears to magically lighten or darken. Josef Albers illustrates the Bezold effect quite simply with an illustration of a brick-colored wall where white mortar raises the value of the red brick and black mortar makes the brickwork appear noticeably darker in value.

To prevent the Bezold effect, strategies can be used to maintain the identity of the color. The designers of oriental rugs selectively outline certain motifs in black to avoid unwanted color interaction. While black outlines create hard boundaries around hues (known as *pronouncement),* white outlines form soft boundaries (called *irradiation)* and create what appears to be a more pliable edge that gives the impression of lightening the surrounding hue. Figures 3-12a, b show how the same color

Top **Figure 3-12a**
Bezold effect in spiral patterns

Bottom **Figure 3-12b**
Bezold effect illustrates a relative value shift by introducing black or white

can be influenced by the addition of either white or black. Notice ways in which visual boundaries in interior architecture separate colors; for example, crown moldings and baseboards, typically painted in shades of white, delineate wall, ceiling, and floor planes.

# Summary

This chapter overviewed the dynamic relationship between light, object, and the visual system that results in color perception. The phenomenon of color constancy indicates that colors appear the same under different lighting conditions. The interaction between color and light, however, sometimes contributes to color illusions and unwanted effects such as metamerism. An exception to color constancy, metamerism occurs when colors match under one light source but change under different lighting conditions.

The visual system also is involved in the perception of color. Color perception involves an electrochemical series of reactions in the eye and brain. Color vision can be measured in color plate tests, offering a pass/fail measure of color vision, and in more precise assessments involving instruments like the Farnsworth-Munsell 100-Hue test. Finally, the chapter described color illusions of successive contrast, simultaneous contrast, transparency, optical mixing, and the Bezold effect.

**NOTES**

1. Kushwah, *Lighting in the Design Process.*
2. Raney, *Color Development.*
3. Zakia, *Perception and Imaging*, 122.

# Color for Preference

*Today we can have our houses and our cars and our clothes any color we like—without any reference to nature or to anything more symbolic than the fashion world's decisions about what colors are "right" for next season.*

—Victoria Finlay

## Color Marketing and Preference Research

The profession of color forecasting for the American consumer market formally began in 1915.[1] To this day, professional groups such as the Color Marketing Group (CMG) and the Color Association of the United States (CAUS) exert a powerful influence on industrial color trends. Color forecasting revolves around the merchandising of products. Because of market availability, color trends undoubtedly influence personal preferences. The harvest golds and avocado greens of the late 1960s and early 1970s

63

produced a widespread groan in the 1980s. Likewise, the mauves and grays of the 1980s appear dated today. Fashion colors and market trends continue to increase color offerings while compressing color cycles. This means more colors go in and out of style at an ever-accelerating pace.[2]

Newness for the sake of newness encourages a throwaway mentality that threatens the world environment. Nearly four decades ago, Victor Papenek argued for "ecologically responsible" design that joins advanced technology with the spirit of craftsmanship.[3] In studying Papenek's substantial contributions to design theory, Rosefelt states, "The recycling of products could reverse this chain of deterioration intrinsically connected to mass-production, back into a new chain of workmanship quality, full use of a product, and reduction of pollution through the reduction of waste."[4] According to this view, designers are accountable for their products.

What does it mean for the environment when people update still-functional interiors every few years? It will be interesting to see whether increased public awareness of sustainability issues can slow color and marketing trends. Preferences for color change evolve over the life span and even from season to season.

An early landmark study on color preference by psychologist Hans Eysenck supported the idea of universal color preferences. Coupling his own experimental findings with an exhaustive survey of over 20,000 studies, he found evidence for general order of color preferences. Regardless of gender, race, or culture, blue is the most preferred hue, followed by red, green, violet, orange, and yellow. This finding was challenged, however, with controls for value and saturation. That is, people usually prefer stronger colors to less saturated ones. Further, general color preferences do not always apply to particular situations. For example, consumers may report that blue is their overall favorite color, but most prefer to buy neutral-colored cars over blue ones.[5]

Why do humans seem to gravitate toward certain colors while avoiding others? Eysenck and other researchers hypothesized a biological basis to color preferences. Developmental research shows that infants appear fascinated by bright, long-wavelength colors, and, until age 6, children tend to favor red, orange, and yellow over cool hues; their preferences then change to blues and greens as they grow older.

What implications do color preferences have for designers? Interior designers have strategies for working with client color preferences that are described in several narratives presented later in this chapter. Skilled designers recognize ways to work with client color preferences without unnecessarily constraining the possible solutions. Further, color preferences do not always generalize across contexts. Even though a client may like a saturated swatch of fabric, it does not mean she would feel comfortable surrounded by this color in her office. Considering preference in relation to other color criteria may be the best process strategy. Figure 4-1 underscores the role of preference in the color planning framework.

Some evidence suggests older adults generally like blues and greens in their residences. However, a segment of this population has difficulty distinguishing between blues and greens of comparable value and intensity, caused by the yellowing of the cornea. For such individuals, closely related blues and greens may prove hazardous in residences or in congregate care facilities. Creating sufficient contrast in value and chroma within the interior color palette offers a safer color solution.

Preferences are not only tied to individuals but also reflect the time, place, and circumstances in which they live. Colors capture the quality of an era, and the popularity of hues changes in periods of war and peace, in economic depression or prosperity. The acceptance of colors correlates with the collective spirit of the day. For example, the colors associated with the Great Depression of the 1920s appear dark and more tonal than the lighter and brighter palettes associated with optimistic times. During the social and political strife of the 1960s and 1970s, popular color

**Figure 4-1**
Color planning framework identifies designer, client, and occupant preferences and market cycles

palettes appeared more strident and edgy than in previous decades. Advances in technology, dyestuffs, and materials also influence the introduction of new colors into the market. For example, the advent of new technologies allowed many more products to be introduced in turquoise blues in the 1950s.

Trends also reflect the signature styles of celebrities, high-profile designers, and artists as well as world events and other newsworthy indicators. For example, Michael Graves created a signature blue that readily identifies his Target product line, just as in the 1940s the well-known designer William Pahlmann created a signature blue-green known as *Pahlmann blue*.[6] The heavy reliance of interior designers on textiles and fabrics creates a fairly close affiliation among interior design, textile design, and the fashion industry.

Color marketing revolves around the merchandising of products and is used in support of social causes—think of Livestrong's yellow rubber wristbands, the red ribbons of AIDS activism, the pink product lines associated with breast cancer awareness. Because market availability controls access to color offerings, at some level color trends undoubtedly influence personal preferences. Recognizing personal color preferences is a form of self-awareness. For example, Figure 4-2 contains two groupings of colors representing a particular individual's preferences. While this design student likes one palette more than the other, either coloration could be successfully integrated into a design.

CMG and CAUS strongly influence the color lines introduced by manufacturers across industries today. Developing color directions and trends by market sector, these organizations survey large consumer groups not only on their preferences but also on their color associations (such as what colors signify power, etc.). A marketing

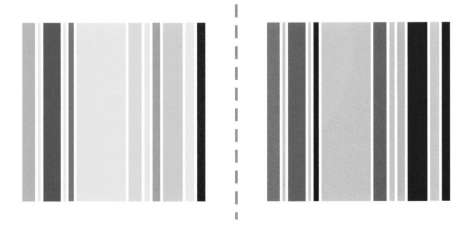

**Figure 4-2**
Example of color preferences of an individual: liked colors (right) and disliked colors (left)

Color Planning for Interiors

research study conducted by one of these organizations may have its participants select from one hundred color cards when answering questions about their color preferences and associations.

In addition to CMG and CAUS, Pantone Color also develops themed palettes to forecast color in design markets. These colorations reflect contemporary lifestyles, pop culture, entertainment, international influences, and social issues. Under the direction of Leatrice Eiseman, its executive director, the Pantone Color Institute produced this forecast for 2007 interior design palettes:[7]

"Fresh Air" presents an imaginative combination of color and texture, including green (green pesto), yellow, pink (cyclamen), purple, violet, blue (sky blue), and white (snow white).

"Classic Chic" combines classical influences with a contemporary feeling. Darker yellows (mineralized yellow), reds (chile pepper), and brown (cappuccino) combine with a range of metallic grays.

"Simply Elegant" reflects a synthesis of modern and traditional influences. Deep brown (mahogany) and purple pair with a range of metallic hues (deep bronze tones).

"Lumens" suggests a full-spectral approach containing hues ranging from waterborne blues, emeralds, and opaline green, ultraviolet, and saturated rose to metallic silvers and bright white.

"Melange" signals a playful combination of orange (apricot, melon), red (strawberry), and yellow tones complemented by a tonal blue-purple (balancing blue) and a yellow-based neutral (khaki).

"Au Naturale" displays an organic quality combining neutrals (creamy whites, sandy beiges, gray, and mellow brown) accented with tonal red (rose), green (lily pad green), and blue (faded denim).

"Grass Roots" has a handcrafted, local-materials flavor featuring yellow and blue-based greens accented by browns (wood tones), purple (grape), and orange (terra cotta).

"Light Touch" presents a high-key palette of softer hues in a modern interpretation containing tints of yellow (sun-tinged yellow), pink, green (foamy aqua), and purple (lavender) mixed with neutrals (champagne or rosy taupe).

What larger themes are expressed in the eight palettes developed by Pantone? Each palette (Figure 4-3) contains seven colors plus neutrals such as whites, grays, and metallic hues. From bronze and copper to gold to silver, metallic surfaces define "Simply Elegant." Cool gray, silver, browns, and the contrast of black and white anchor "Classic Chic." Each palette includes neutrals or exceedingly tonal hues that enhance the main hues.

Developing sensitivity to the influence of neutral colors, especially in conjunction with textural contrast, sets the groundwork for elegance and sophistication. An analysis of the 2007 Pantone Forecast suggests the integral relationship of color and texture. Palettes are described with words like *luminous, shiny, metallic sheen, de-lustered,* and *unbleached quality.* The surface quality, whether highly reflective or matte in finish, influences the feel and quality of the overall palette. A beautiful neutral palette can shape the spatial envelope and communicate the quality of a refined, airy, and light interior.

Within tonal palettes, designers typically create textural variety in surface quality to avoid prosaic and monotonous interiors. With strong color contrast, whites or other neutrals can balance the chroma level. A polychromatic or full-spectrum palette appears harmonious when a generous amount of white is introduced. Another strategy in working with color is to control the value or key of the specified colors. This is evidenced in the Pantone scheme "Light Touch," which consists of tints mixed from a white base. These related hues create a high-key palette of similar values, while the low-key "Lumens" palette emphasizes shades of blues, greens, and silvers.

# Stories Behind Color Names

Studying the names of colors and the stories behind their origins offers fascinating insight into color meaning. Many color names tell a story, according to color scholar Jeannie Heifetz. Her etymological investigation into nearly two hundred color names revealed their origins in all corners of the globe and that color names with staying power continue to enter languages. Her investigation discovered color names

**Figure 4-3**
Example of a 2007 Pantone color palette

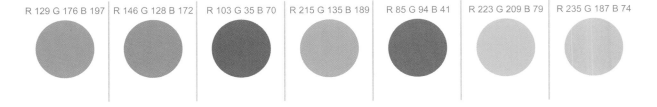

R 129 G 176 B 197    R 146 G 128 B 172    R 103 G 35 B 70    R 215 G 135 B 189    R 85 G 94 B 41    R 223 G 209 B 79    R 235 G 187 B 74

Color Planning for Interiors

derived from "gemstones, metals, spices, wines, fruits, flowers, plants, woods, birds, animals (as well as colors we use only for animals), fossils, the earth, people, cities, and even a battle."[8] A sampling of color names and origins researched by Heifetz appears in Figure 4-4.

Snow white (1000, Anglo-Saxon)—color of material
Violet (1370, Latin)—color of the flower
Orange (1512, Persian)—color of the fruit
Copper (1594, Greek)—color of metal
Sky blue (1728, Old Norse and Sanskrit)—color of the sky
Khaki (1848, Hindi)—color of dust
Terra cotta (1882, Italian)—color of pottery
Champagne (1915, French and Latin)—color of the beverage

Color language evolved across history and culture as people interacted in their environments. Interestingly, the name *snow white*, which appeared in a recent Pantone color forecast, originally was used by Anglo-Saxons over a thousand years ago. Less than a hundred years ago, *champagne* as a color word entered the French language; it comes from the Champagne region of France, which produces the grapes for champagne. Heifetz discovered the story behind the naming of *khaki*, a Hindi word meaning "earth or dust." In the mid-1800s, British soldiers deployed to India wore dusty tan uniforms to camouflage themselves in the face of sniper attacks. Their original white uniforms were dyed with a mixture of mud, tea leaves, coffee, and ink now known as *khaki*. When schooled in the history of color words, designers can develop meaningful design concepts with color stories that speak to a sense of place in culturally sensitive ways. Of course, expressive meaning can be coupled with compositional and other color criteria to create an integrated design.

Returning to the 2007 Pantone Forecast as an example, many of the color names relate to the natural environment, and the names of the hues reference broad categories of materials (natural and fabricated), food, and fabric.

**Figure 4-4**
Example of color names and origins

| Violet | Orange | Copper | Sky Blue | Khaki | Terra Cotta | Champagne |
|---|---|---|---|---|---|---|
| 1370; Latin | 1512; Persian | 1594; Greek | 1728; Old Norse; Sanskrit | 1848; Hindi | 1882; Italian | 1915; Latin |

The Pantone-specific color names for this palette appear in parentheses.

**Natural Materials**
    Wood (mahogany)
    Metals (gold, silver, bronze, copper)
    Flora (cyclamen pink, lavender, poppy red, rose, violet, lily pad green)
    Gemstones (emerald)
    Other (sky blue, sun-tinged yellow, sand, snow white)

**Fabricated Materials**
    Textiles (denim, khaki)
    Pottery (terra cotta)

**Foods**
    Fruits (apricot, grape, melon, orange, strawberry)
    Spice and seasoning (chile pepper, green pesto)
    Drinks (cappuccino, champagne)

To better understand concepts of color communication in interior design practice, the following project narrative describes how a designer can work with client preferences in relation to other color planning criteria. Notice the words such as *marsh green* and *cinnabar red* that the designer uses to communicate about color with her client.

# Cinnabar: Residential Design

Noted residential designer Phyllis Taylor believes color is as essential to interior design as is structure. Recently, Taylor worked with a client who professed not to like color, much less color trends. This client also feared committing to a color direction and then tiring of it. Yet Taylor persisted in learning about the client and her sensibilities, which included an affinity with nature. Armed with this insight, Taylor incorporated tonal greens into the space using a hue she referred to as *marsh green,* and this color helped create a tranquil sense of place, particularly in the private areas of the condominium. The client also preferred light wood, and Taylor selected a natural saw-cut white oak for the flooring. The client agreed that the light-colored, quartersawn wood complemented the palette (Figure 4-5a).

*Opposite*
**Figure 4-5a**
Client preference for
colors and materials

**Figure 4-5b**

Neutral flooring and
textural contrast

Carpet marked another early design decision (Figure 4-5b). The client preferred neutral carpeting, described by Taylor as neither gray nor brown. When working with clients who are intimidated by color, Taylor recommends creating strong textural variation as a good substitute for color contrast. We see this principle at play in the half-bath, where a large-scale, hollowed African log creates a concave backdrop to an oval mirror and a black granite pedestal fixture (Figure 4-5c).

*Opposite*
**Figure 4-5c**

Textural emphasis in
neutral palette

The client found this unique piece on one of her travels to Africa, and Taylor considered several installation possibilities for it before deciding on its final destination. The carved ribs in the wood create a strong rhythm and contrast with the smoothness of the mirror, stone, and metal.

*Top* **Figure 4-5d**
Cinnabar red in
dining space

*Bottom* **Figure 4-5e**
Optical mixing in tile
backsplash implies
abstract animal print

Taylor wanted to expand the palette for the interior. She discovered the client had several items of red clothing in her largely taupe and black wardrobe. Red also surfaced in the client's collection of artifacts from Africa and Asia. Red proved to be the bridge color in the interior. As trust between the client and designer grew, Taylor made the case for the selective use of an intense red, or *cinnabar*, in high-impact spaces. For Taylor, the psychological effect of a saturated red is invigorating; she recalls an early memory of a nearly luminous red space that was simply powerful. In this case, Taylor limited red to the more public areas of the condominium. In the living room, red balances large, fairly neutral furniture and artwork and contributes energy to the spaces for entertaining and dining (Figure 4-5d). In the kitchen, Taylor designed a mosaic backsplash, reinforcing the African theme, using four types of marble tile that optically mix into an abstract animal print (Figure 4-5e).

**Figure 4-5f**
Desaturated hues in master bedroom

The proportion of color distinguishes the public, semiprivate, and private spaces of the residence. The private areas contain much less red. The master bedroom and bath are mostly neutral, with accents of tonal greens and desaturated reds (Figures 4-5f, g). The hallway leading to the guest rooms was designed to be an inviting destination. A circular African feather headdress creates a striking focal point against a bronze wall and is lit by two MR16 lamps, while recessed spots act as wall washers

(Figure 4-5h). The metallic brown complements the red Asian chest in a way black walls could not. Taylor warns that black paint tends to dissolve planar surfaces in interiors by acting as a visual vacuum, absorbing all light. Dark metallic paint colors, such as the bronze, also can be quite reflective, a factor that enhances the headdress. Taylor might have opted for a red rather than a neutral wall if the client were more comfortable with hue and chroma; however, in this case, she decided that the red headdress would itself contribute visual interest to the transition space.

From day to night, colors in an interior can change, sometimes dramatically. Initially, this posed a problem in the living room, where white mullions appeared as a string of vertical bars over the windows at night. To convince the client that this contrast threatened to eclipse the design of the space, Taylor brought her to the under-construction interior at night to show the unwanted effect. The client decided to have the mullions repainted at considerable expense using an electrostatic painting process with a powder-coat finish. The resulting bronze hue harmonizes with the interior under both day and night conditions (Figure 4-5i). Taylor observes that even in a single room, a paint color can appear to change from wall plane to wall plane. This effect reminds her of Josef Albers's classic color illusions, to which she was first introduced as an interior design student.

**Figure 4-5h**
Red creates a focal point in African feather headdress

Color was considered early in the design process. Conceptualizing the spatial envelope through a circular process of sketching, perspective studies, and computer renderings, Taylor worked through design ideas with the client, who had trouble

Figure 4-5i
Neutral window
mullions do not attract
attention in either
nighttime or daylight
conditions

visualizing the space. After Taylor developed the basic scheme of green and red with neutrals, she refined the color selections by testing wall color options on-site. Potential hues were then painted onto 30 × 40-inch foam-core boards and viewed against different wall surfaces in the day and evening to narrow the color choices. The next step involved painting areas of color onto the walls to make final on-site adjustments. For an award-winning designer like Taylor, viewing samples of paint and fabrics in her own office, even under several lighting settings, cannot replace on-site testing and refinement.

# Firehouse Red: Adaptive Use

Taylor recalls working with another client who fully embraced saturated color, and red became the obvious choice for his adaptive reuse of a firehouse (Figure 4-6a). In this redux, the main floor of the firehouse had ample space to display and work on the client's high-performance cars, while the second floor offered space for entertaining. From the onset, Taylor immediately began associating red with fire and the client's Ferrari Testarossa, a sportscar whose name translates to "redhead." The client quickly embraced the idea of incorporating red throughout the interior (Figure 4-6b). Additionally, Taylor introduced a dark yellow paint finish into the palette with a matte brushed-aluminum finish (Figure 4-6c). The metallic element signifies a technological aesthetic, while the yellow Solar-Ray paint symbolizes the sun's heat with a tonality that compositionally grounds the palette (Figures 4-6d, e). Taylor notes the challenge of mixing yellow paint to a desired effect, referring to this hue as "volatile."

Color preference, both client likes and dislikes, surfaced in these residential projects; however, client preference can come into play in commercial design too, as illustrated in the next narrative.

**Figure 4-6a**
Firehouse adaptive use

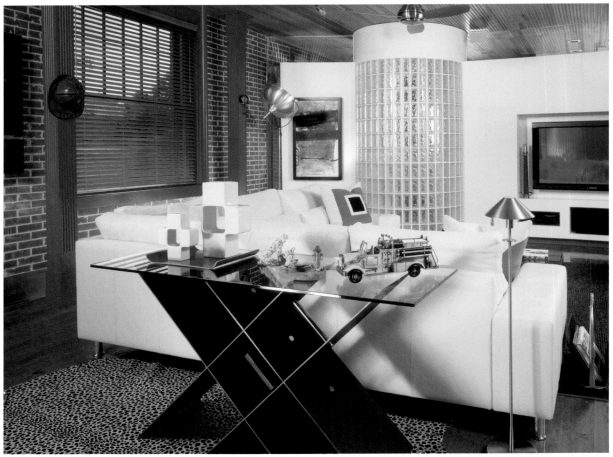

*Opposite*
*Top Left* **Figure 4-6b**
Interior houses car
collection

*Top Right* **Figure 4-6c**
Red, dark yellow,
and aluminum
finishes create
interior coloration

*Bottom* **Figure 4-6d**
Incorporation of white
within palette

**Figure 4-6e**
Color palette
unifies private and
public spaces

*Color for Preference*

# Kiwi and Tangerine: Workplace

This case describes the design of a small office, underscoring the objective and subjective aspects of color. As an orientation, the interior color pattern is described objectively, followed by the process account of the client's subjective color response. The orientation to the case and narrative were researched and developed by Laura Compton Busse as part of a master's thesis project I supervised; they are used with permission.

The Munsell notations for the colors specified in this workplace design appear in Figure 4-7. An early phase of color planning involved selecting greens and oranges from commercial textile lines. These hues were then narrowed to choices in closer

| | COLOR | MUNSELL NOTATION | APPLICATION |
|---|---|---|---|
| RECEPTION | | 7.5PB 4/10 | Pendant Lamps |
| | | 2.5GY 6/4 | Accent Wall |
| | | 2.5YR 6/8 | Accent Wall |
| | | 5Y 7/2 | Ceiling and Structure |
| CONFERENCE | | 2.5YR 6/8 | Accent Wall |
| | | 5Y 7/2 | Wall and Structure |
| | | 5BG 4/2 | Furniture |
| OFFICE | | 2.5YR 6/8 | Accent Wall |
| | | 2.5GY 6/4 | Accent Wall |
| | | 5Y 7/2 | Ceiling and Workstation |

**Figure 4-7**
Munsell notation in office, conference, and reception spaces

value and chroma ranges. In its final form, the palette contained three dominant hues: a bluish green, a reddish orange, and a yellow-green, plus a complex yellow-based neutral and a blue-purple.

The chroma of the purple-blue is much stronger than the other hues and functions as a surprise accent in the interior. The limited number of hues and the narrow range in value unifies the small office. The complex neutral chosen for the window walls frames the exterior view of the river and downtown. Importantly, it works across seasons with the changing colors in nature. This case describes a design project where the designer gains the trust of the client during the design process. The client's color preferences come into play, as do compositional, behavioral, and pragmatic considerations. The client and designer reviewed the case and approved the narrative for accuracy.

This 1,725-square-foot space is located near the top of a fifteen-story neoclassical building built in 1915. The small workplace houses a nonprofit organization with an executive director and several employees. In addition, the workplace must accommodate visitor groups for meetings. The space requirements include a private office, systems furniture, a conference space, a work room, and kitchen and storage areas. Color preference was a pivotal issue because the client had to be convinced to move beyond personal color preferences. Tensions in the color planning process revolved around the color choices for the interior walls.

Other color criteria factored into the design process as well. Space planning for the limited square footage led to a unique interaction of color and form. Creating an exciting design image in the office was critical because the organization is affiliated with the interior design industry. Pragmatic issues affected the design solution as well. All these issues surface in the narrative "Beyond the Comfort Zone," written by Laura Compton Busse.

## *Beyond the Comfort Zone*

A certain balance between trust and personal preference defines the relationship between an expert and a client. "Green and orange! My thirty-year-old kitchen is green and orange!" The client reacted strongly to the color palette proposed for the new office. The interior designer for the project quickly responded, "Oh, no, not *that* kind of green and orange. I was thinking a *tangerine* orange with a *kiwi* green." The client's anxiety abated as the visions of pea-green workstations disappeared. As in the restaurant industry, presentation and careful attention to semantics are critical. Which sounds more palatable, snails or escargot? Squid or calamari? What does the client need, and how can it be delivered to ensure acceptance?

The client organization's prominent place in the design community brings a steady stream of visitors and volunteers with high expectations to its headquarters. Much time was invested in choosing the perfect location for a new office that would be less expensive to lease. The proposed site for renovation, only three blocks from the old location, was smaller in square footage and required a total gutting. Settling on a location and starting to review initial space plans gave the client confidence that the final outcome would be successful.

The color planning began in earnest with the designer's assurance that the final design would reinforce mission and identity for the organization. Both client and designer wanted the interior design in the new office to set a standard of excellence.

The project designer, who joined the project after the initial schematics, carefully studied the feedback from a one-day charette involving the architect, organizational board members, and employees. The employees had gathered photographs in advance; with the larger group, they created a list of words symbolic of the proposed space. The result was a photo collage of magazine clippings depicting appealing spaces. It is interesting to note that a year later, when the client and employees thought back on the design process, they hinted the final design did not really reflect the original collage, which showed spaces with natural light and earthy textures and materials. Imagine ordering an entree that comes out different than anticipated but is still satisfying.

This process left the client wondering, "Was the designer considering our input, or were these just the colors she felt like using?" but conceded the project was no easy task. Downsizing from 2,500 square feet to just over 1,700, working within the confines of a historic building, and the goal of achieving a fresh, unexpected design all influenced the project. Designing under these many constraints can be likened to creating an innovative vegan meal.

The client's professional contacts and the systems furniture donation provided the springboard for the palette. Using the given furniture finishes narrowed the options in the process of selecting the neutral putty color. Finding several swatches of green and orange in textiles spurred the designer to consider the psychological effects of these colors: calming and relaxing, but bold enough to be energizing. While persuading the client of the merits of the proposed palette, the designer contemplated the other issues affecting the design—systems furniture with full-height partitions, the cubic space, and the substantial amount of natural light in the space.

Although the client and the employees were open to fresh ideas for their image, their initial reaction to the proposed palette was less than enthusiastic. The client remembers her apprehension: "It would have been fine to do the burnt orange and leave the green out, or do the green and just the putty. But when you put those colors together, they were like, what are you doing? What are you doing?" Most important, would the colors reflect the organizational mission? During this process, the client had not confronted her personal preferences. She gravitated toward blues and purples, yet the designer forcefully argued for the green and orange palette. How would the designer convince her client of the merits of this color direction?

Construction of the office began, and soon drywall was installed. Being only three blocks away gave the client and the other employees plenty of opportunity to watch the project evolve. Upon viewing the gutted space with only drywall partitions, the stark white walls appeared too bright, almost overpowering, in the natural light that flooded the space from large windows on two walls. "It was truly uncomfortable in there with those white walls, and not particularly friendly or inviting," reflects the client. As the construction unfolded, the client's trust in the designer grew, but she remained concerned about how the final color scheme would come together. How would the color palette translate to the space? The designer's careful attention to detail was apparent in the color development as she honed the value and chroma of the hues.

The final design exceeded expectations in every sense, including the client's appreciation for a new and different color palette. The client summarizes, "I guess the big thing for me is that the color, it seems to me, does a great deal to enhance the design of the space. If you look at the layout of the space, you can see all these angles that radiate from the entry door to the windows. And it seems to me that the colors support those lines. The color helps set off the various angles."

What can be learned from this experience? The way a designer presents a color scheme can determine its acceptance. Suggestions from a designer may not be the personal choice of the client, but the design must consider not only the employee perspective but also the company itself. A successful designer gets to know the client, establishes trust, and develops insights into the intangibles related to the organization. Sometimes insights originate with persons outside the organization who have the expertise to communicate a message visually. The restaurant patron does not pay the chef the price of the raw ingredients. Rather, the patron pays for the chef's professional experience, including knowledge, education, and ability to innovate. The relationship of client and expert fundamentally requires trust. When a designer establishes an atmosphere of trust, she enables the client to move beyond her comfort zone toward the innovative and exciting.

### Color Interpretation

The color planning decisions in this project relate to preference, communication, composition, and pragmatics, and they speak to a growing trust between the client and designer. The final award-winning office interior communicates the organizational mission in no uncertain terms. Both visitors and employees believe the interior achieved lofty project goals. Even at the small scale of the space, the color communicates a progressive aesthetic. Further, the designer significantly influenced perception of the space through the use of bold color on the interior, angled walls, and neutral coloration on the exterior window walls. The contribution of neutral hues to the color scheme may be overlooked, but they offer visual relief from the more saturated hues. Color continuity on the interior walls enlivens the work areas, while the window views relax and calm. The small space feels larger than it is because of the space planning and coloration. From a pragmatic standpoint, new systems furniture was donated to the project. These work surfaces and storage units were available in a set range of colors and finishes and therefore also influenced the interior coloration.

# Color Marketing: Model Condominium

This example describes a condominium project that was not tailored to an individual or a family but rather was designed with the intent of appealing to a particular demographic market: young adults attracted to a downtown, urban lifestyle. Senior principal Larry Wilson of Rink Design Partnership, Inc., who spearheaded this project and created its custom wall sculpture, emphatically states, "This was not to be your father's condo." The interior orange and green create contrast and feel youthful. Color offers a tool to explicitly help direct prospective buyers from the first floor of the condominium into the upper loft and bedroom spaces. Within the loft, a strategically placed red Eames chair entices visitors down the hallway.

Color planning is a form of creative problem-solving that can be cultivated by experiences outside the field of interior design. For example, ideas of line, contrast, and space underlyingthe dragonwood sculptures created by Wilson (Figure 4-10) later inspired custom pieces for several interior spaces he was designing (Figures 4-8a–d). Likewise, Wilson's paintings, such as "Rising Above" from the Ediface series in Figure 4-9, explore color and spatial relationships in ways he believes profoundly influence his thinking about architectural color. Wilson's idea bank is most synergistic when his design and art reinforce and inform one another.

*Opposite*
**Figure 4-8a**
Example of interior coloration tailored to young urban professionals

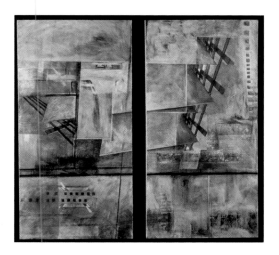

# Summary

Color preferences represent more than an individual's simple likes or dislikes. At its best, the study of color preferences advances the understanding of human proclivities at different points in time and across different cultures; at its worst, color preference, particularly the accelerating cycle of fashion colors, is the antithesis of sustainable design. Both personal preferences and market-driven trends may influence the color planning process. Recognizing designer, client, consumer, and market preferences and directions helps in better understanding the client perspective and suggests ways to support individuality and timelessness.

*Opposite*

*Top Left* **Figure 4-8b**
Color contrast
defines loft space

*Top Right* **Figure 4-8c**
Color unifies and also
separates public from
private spaces

*Bottom* **Figure 4-8d**
Red Eames chair
draws attention
and directs visitors
through the hallway

*Above*

*Top Left* **Figure 4-9**
Edifice series, "Rising
Above," mixed media
over plaster on wood
panels, each panel
24 × 48 × 3.5 inches

*Top Right* **Figure 4-10**
Old Growth series,
"Transept Shelter with
Orbs," dragonwood,
stainless steel, and tie
wire, 10 feet in diam-
eter, 12 feet in height

## RESEARCH NOTES

Empirical studies of color preferences were begun in the late nineteenth century. The initial outpouring of such research has subsided somewhat over time due to shortcomings in defining, explaining, and measuring color preferences.[9] Critics often cite the narrow focus of such studies as problematic, with many researchers simply asking study participants to report their favorite color or colors by preference without explaining the underlying meaning of their findings. Further, the results of some color preference studies can be challenged in terms of their methodology. When color samples are inconsistent, research results cannot be trusted. It is difficult to compare findings on preference across studies testing color preference with colored paper, fabric, light, digital stimuli, or color names.

*continues*

## RESEARCH NOTES *continued*

Too often, researchers limit their testing to highly saturated hues; however, recent studies appear to be controlling for some of these problems by using standardized systems, such as Munsell, to numerically specify hue, value, and intensity in the test materials for evaluation. Other variables to be controlled when researching color preference are the light source for viewing colors and the screening of color vision in the test subjects. In sum, the object, the light, and the perceiver all must be carefully and consistently controlled in color preference research to yield valid and reliable findings.

### NOTES

1. Hope and Walch, *The Color Compendium.*
2. Ibid.
3. Papenek, *Design for the Real World.*
4. Rosefelt, *The Design Dilemma*, 245.
5. Eysenck, "A Critical and Experimental Study of Color Preferences."
6. Tate and Smith, *Interior Design in the 20th Century.*
7. Pantone Matching System,© *COLORINSPIRATION/2007,* swatch book.
8. Heifetz, *When Blue Meant Yellow,* 8.
9. Rapoport and Rapoport, "Color Preferences, Color Harmony, and Quantitative Use of Color."

# Color Composition

*While color appears to lie on the surface, it is not superficial. It signals a sense of space, or assigns form in perception, and connotes meaning by association.*

—Lois Swirnoff

Designers use color as a compositional element to unify, create focal points, and develop spatial relationships. Composition—the integration of color and form—is the central function in the color planning framework (Figure 5-1).

## Color-Form Relationships

Artist and professor Lois Swirnoff has observed, created, taught, and written about color-form relationships since studying under Josef Albers in the 1950s. Her book *Dimensional Color* contains a particularly striking series of transformations where

color dramatically alters the appearance of a three-dimensional model.[1,2] Some colorations appear to change the three-dimensional appearance of the model, while others visually flatten the structure, making it seem two-dimensional. Composed of two cubes joined by a common base, the model is never altered; only its applied color changes. By closely studying the highlights and shadows of the form, color can be carefully selected and applied to either reinforce or contradict its planar edges. When the applied color bisects the surface planes, the geometry appears to change even though the model remains constant throughout the series of color illusions. The manipulation of value alone also appears to dramatically alter the form. This demonstration powerfully illustrates the potential of color in interior architecture. Figure 5-2 illustrates my students' interpretation of this study.

# Value Relationships

In his quest for precision in color communication, Albert Munsell was first to use the term *value* to describe the lightness or darkness of a color. Scientists estimate humans are able to distinguish twelve or thirteen shades of gray. Humans can easily discrimi-

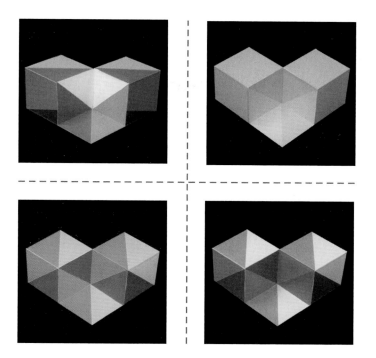

**Figure 5-2**
Color-form interaction illustrating transformations of a model through systematic manipulations

nate lighter grays and whites but have more difficulty seeing variations in darker grays and blacks. This can easily be demonstrated by mixing a gray scale with paint or digitally preparing an equally gradated series of grays that progress from white to black. This exercise takes patience because it is difficult to create distinct, evenly spaced gradations, especially in the darker range of the scale. Greater value intervals or steps in the darker regions prevent the intervals from visually blending.

The Munsell system contains a ten-step value scale consisting of visually equal steps ranging from black to white. Numerically pure black equals 1, and white equals 10. The primary triad on the artists' wheel would translate into the following values: yellow is a light value (7), red is a midrange value (5), and blue represents a dark value (2). The value of the color can be lightened by mixing white into the hue, creating a tint. A very light blue tint can be equal in value to a primary yellow, translating into a light gray (7). Adjusting the primary hues to a similar value level lessens the contrast in this color scheme. The value of a hue is lowered by adding black, creating a shade. A primary yellow quickly mixes into a yellow-green hue when mixed with black. Unlike value, hue and chroma do not have achromatic counterparts. Figure 5-3 illustrates a value scale.

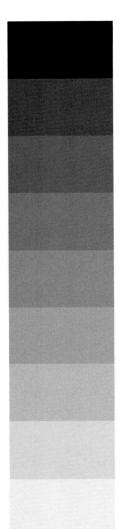

Color palettes with similar values can be compared to harmonious musical chords. The overall value of the color palette is the value key. A low-key (dark) palette contains values 1–3, while a high-key (pastel) palette consists of values 7–10. Midrange palettes are in the 4–6 value range. Just as a song can be played in a certain key, a color scheme can be translated into a high, medium, or low key. For example, a high-key palette of pale yellow, pink, and blue appears much lighter in value than lower-key colors of ocher, burgundy, and navy.

Why is value critical to consider when planning color in interiors? Value affects the perceived scale and spatial relationship of the interior, where lighter colors appear more visually expansive than darker ones, which often seem to compress space. Contrast levels can align with the design intent. To create a more unified appearance, the designer may want to develop a palette with closely related values; however, to emphasize spatial character, greater contrast of values can be introduced in the selected colors.

Each color in the visual spectrum has its own spectral value. The reflected wavelengths of yellow make this hue inherently lighter in value and brighter than blue, while the spectral values of red and green are similar. This natural phenomenon is reflected in the three-dimensional form of the Munsell solid, which is irregular rather than perfectly spherical. Some artists deliberately shift the inherent value of hues in their palettes. This practice, known as *color inversion,* appears in several paintings from Georgia O'Keeffe's floral series.[3] For example, the greens appear notably darker than the red-violet in *White Iris,* painted in 1926. In this painting, the spectral value relationship between green and purple is inverted. This coloration underscores the imaginative magnification of the single iris. Decades later, in *Poppies,* which O'Keeffe completed in 1950, the oranges and reds of the flowers appear much darker in value than the blue sky. This use of color inversion emphasizes detail and the form of the poppies.

## Value Relationships in Interiors

According to Harold Linton, "Following the establishment of tonal patterns in design, variations in hue and chroma can be considered in relation to an existing plan."[4] Value occupies a central position in shaping interior space. Figures 5-4a–c illustrate three restaurant interiors that are high key in value. These interiors feel light and spacious. When hue and chroma are restrained, texture assumes greater importance. Sheer fabric panels, light leather, pale tone-on-tone carpet patterns, and a dragonwood screen express sophisticated materiality in an understated, high-key palette.

**Figure 5-3**
Value gradation
(nine steps)

*Opposite*
**Figure 5-4a**
High-key interior with
fabric room dividers

Color Planning for Interiors

*Top* **Figure 5-4b**
High-key interior where banquette seat and back cushions vary in value based on functionality

*Bottom* **Figure 5-4c**
Dragonwood screen adds textural interest in a neutral limited palette

Color Planning for Interiors

In comparison, the darker interiors in Figures 5-5a, b appear visually heavy, although the lighting and introduction of some lighter materials add much-needed contrast. The black ceiling appears to dissolve and redirects attention to the pattern and lighting in the interior. The designer of this space, Larry Wilson, prefers to specify a warm black when the overall material palette is warm and a cool black when the material palette is cool. Substituting a very dark hue for the black produces similar but chromatically more complex solutions. For example, a dark red-purple ceiling could be used in an upscale food market. This hue would reflect more light and not appear harsh in the setting.

Dark values also can be employed on planar wall, ceiling, and floor surfaces to great effect. Figure 5-5b shows two mirrors that appear to be suspended from a wall surface. The dark value of the wall sets the stage for a floating illusion wherein the mirrors appear magically suspended. In this interior, patrons come into close proximity with the mirrors and are able to appreciate the texture and color variation in the wall's slate tiles. Alternatively, a painted black wall surface would not offer nearly the same level of visual interest.

Figures 5-6a, b present two interiors, identical except for one color dimension: value. Applying different values to the same space alters the interior composition and feeling. The lighter spa interior appears larger in scale than the darker one. Further, the lighter interior features understated textural variations in the wall plane that are less noticeable in the nearly black tiles in the darker interior. The introduction of a contrasting value visually divides the wall in the darker interior roughly into thirds, forming a rectangular shape that visually recedes and aligns with the whirlpool. Further, the darker wood

**Figure 5-5a**
Black visually dissolves ceiling plane

ceiling visually lowers the ceiling height, intensifying the sense of enclosure when compared to the sister space. The gray tiles surrounding the ledge of the whirlpool help define a physical level change, creating a visual signal that may help prevent falls.

The two interiors are designed for different users; the light space is exclusively for women, the darker space for men. Value not only visually alters the interior but also signals femininity and masculinity. One way to develop compositionally is to experiment with spatial effects by changing value relationships in the same design.

# Color Progression and Transition

From a compositional perspective, color within interior environments can be studied on at least three levels:

- complexity in a single color
- color interactions within a palette
- color relationships within a three-dimensional context

Color relationships within interiors involve time and space, progression and transition. A feeling of movement can be emphasized by systematically sequencing color

*Opposite*
**Figure 5-5b**
Slate wall creates floating mirror illusion and offers textural interest

*Above*
*Left* **Figure 5-6a**
Spa interior, designed for women, appears visually lighter than its counterpart

*Right* **Figure 5-6b**
Spa interior, designed for men, appears visually heavier than its counterpart

along one or more of its dimensions. By creating what professor and artist David Hornung calls a *hue continuum,* color can appear to move across the spectrum from reds to oranges, yellows, greens, and blues to purples.[5] Likewise, a value continuum involves progressions from light to dark, while a saturation continuum moves from one complementary color to another, shifting through complementary gray. Digital progression exercises appear in Figure 5-7, and Figure 5-8 illustrates painted explorations of limited palettes.

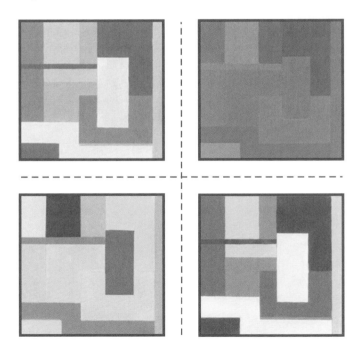

Color Planning for Interiors

## Color Progression and Transition in Interiors

Color can enliven transitional spaces through which people move en route to their destinations. For example, O'Hare Airport in Chicago contains an automated walkway between American Airlines terminals 1 and 2. Murphy/Jahn designed the transitional space with kinetic optical lights that pulsate in rhythm with music. This unfolding of spectral color-sound wraps around the walls and ceilings of the space and makes the transit time seem shorter. With increasing travel security and inconveniences, this may be one of the few airport experiences that reduce the stress of travel. Another example of a spectral continuum was the installation *Harmonic Runway* by Christopher Janney, in the Miami International Airport (Figure 5-9). This passageway, created with angled mirrors and colored light, was filled with the sounds of native birds. Unfortunately, the installation no longer exists, a victim of new construction.

**Figure 5-9**
Miami International Airport transition space illustrating color progression (demolished)

# Integrated Color: Workplace

This project illustrates color composition and progression in two research and development buildings for the Atlanta-based BellSouth Corporation. The Atlanta offices of tvsdesign and HOK collaborated on the design for BellSouth's science and technology group. The intent was to consolidate the company's large employee base into business centers adjacent to the city's metro rail stations, promoting employee mass transit commuting and, ultimately, stronger community engagement. Establish-

ing a relationship between the architecture and the surrounding urban context became paramount in designing the Midtown BellSouth project.

Further, the workplace was to be functional, flexible, and fun. The expansive scope of work for the two buildings included a conference center, meeting spaces, a cafeteria, workstations, and a connector space with a central staircase traversing the buildings. The connector area, with its boat-shaped curve, offered a dynamic pivot point between the buildings and an elegant nexus for small, informal gatherings and larger presentations.

In this project, illustrated in Figures 5-10a–k, color acted to unify, create progressions, and spatially zone the large building complex on several levels. The exterior glass walls of the building appear to radiate from within; a glowing red visually connects with passersby and contrasts with the neighboring cityscape (see Figures 5-10a, b).

This saturated band extends about 300 feet and couples with a secondary striped band, which combines the red hue with a more tonal yellow, orange, and green. Similar in value and chroma, these hues visually remain on the same band, preventing vibration between color adjacencies. A large-scale exercise in color theory, this band wonderfully illustrates many of Itten's color contrasts and directs the eye through the interior space.

As the color progresses into less public areas, the red banding leads to a more complex color and materials palette. For example, the large cafeteria space features red with a tonal blue-green as a complementary partner. The blue-green creates a subdued foil for the seating and carpeted area of the cafeteria. The introduction of a more intense green into the space would have created optical vibrations from the highly saturated complements of red and green. The continuous red wall surface in the cafeteria is punctuated by magnifications of broadband data streams scaled to the wall; these 4 × 6-foot art pieces reflect the research and development core of the organization (see Figures 5-10c, d).

Red continues in the self-service area of the cafeteria as one hue in a tile mosaic of greens and neutrals. This vibrant wall pattern introduces pattern in the space (Figures 5-10e, f).

*Left* **Figure 5-10c**
BellSouth chromatic band

*Right* **Figure 5-10d**
BellSouth digital art

*Color Composition*     105

In other transitional spaces, the coloration appears more neutral with red-toned wood, glass, and metallic finishes. The color temperature is markedly cooler (see Figures 5-10g–i).

Deeper in the building, employees congregate in an informal gathering space formed by a large tonal green wall plane with frosted glass, backlit with colored lights. Green assumes a defining role in this area, while red becomes the ceiling color. The green tone seems appropriate for the individual reflection or quiet conversation that might occur here. Heightening the feeling of calm, the frosted glass contributes a soft glow of color (Figure 5-10j). Finally, in a large conference room, color becomes more subdued to support the lower lighting levels required by the meetings and presentations that take place in this space (Figure 5-10k).

In this project, the design team manipulated color both to create outside engagement and to support internal focus within the organization. The formal quality of color created passageways throughout the building and contributed to the design of the buildings by:

- Creating a connection with the urban setting
- Developing a sense of progression within the interior
- Unifying spaces and creating areas of emphasis
- Communicating energy and corporate mission
- Forming spatial zones by activity and function

*Opposite*
**Figure 5-10j**
BellSouth tonal green gathering space features red ceiling and colored backlit panels

*Above*
**Figure 5-10k**
BellSouth neutralized ballroom space uses limited color to divide floor plane

## Kinetic Color: Workplace

**Figure 5-11a**
SJ Berwin law
firm headquarters
(London)

Color offers a different type of impact in the case of the London headquarters of
the law firm SJ Berwin (Figures 5-11a–g). The result resembles an art gallery or
a boutique hotel. For this project, color and light helped redefine the conventional
image of the legal profession. Design became an explicit tool for recruiting young
legal talent through the new space, which merged three offices into the newly
formed European headquarters.

**Figure 5-11b**
SJ Berwin
reception space
with red lighting

In designing the 250,000-square-foot building,
the designers at HOK created glowing, colored
forms through wall planes and backlit niches that
offer dynamic chroma throughout the austere
and futuristic spaces. The interior architecture
is predominately concrete gray and contains an
abundance of glass, minimalistic furnishings,
and non-objective artwork. Similar to the design
strategy in BellSouth, bands of color create areas
of emphasis in this workplace. However, these
color bands are smaller in scale and are formed
through additive and subtractive color. For example,

*Top* **Figure 5-11c**
SJ Berwin reception
space with purple
lighting

*Bottom* **Figure 5-11d**
SJ Berwin conference
room niche with blue
lighting

*Opposite*
**Figure 5-11e**
SJ Berwin confer-
ence room niche with
yellow-orange lighting

*Top* **Figure 5-11f**
SJ Berwin reception
space, impact of
chromatic artwork

*Bottom* **Figure 5-11g**
SJ Berwin materiality
and color

*Color Composition*          111

each conference space contains a glowing band of colored light; the radiating red-colored light appears much more intense than the blue light (Figures 5-11d, e). A chromatic painting forms a narrow spectral band in one reception space, and this relatively slender linear form helps humanize the scale of the large interior (Figure 5-11f).

The grays of the workplace echo the tonality of the Thames River and St. Paul's Cathedral, visible from the interior perimeter of the building. The entire interior is wireless and contains many informal workspaces outside of individual offices. Explicitly designed with younger attorneys in mind, this firm attracts those who are interested in openness, collaboration, and community in their work lives. Ultimately, the design speaks to a new way of practicing law.

# Summary

This chapter discusses ways color acts compositionally in designed spaces. Color has the ability to transform the apparent structure of two-dimensional and three-dimensional designs through the careful manipulation of hue, value, and chroma. Considering value in relation to form is particularly significant when designing interiors. Typically, humans can distinguish twelve or thirteen differences in value; lighter values are easier to distinguish than darker ones. Each hue has its own spectral value indicating its natural lightness and brightness. Color gradations in hue, value, and saturation can be studied on two-dimensional surfaces and in three-dimensional space. Color progression relates to the dimensions of time and space. The chapter concludes with two workplace projects that clearly demonstrate purposeful treatments of compositional color.

**NOTES**

1. Swirnoff, *Dimensional Color*.
2. Swirnoff, "Experiments on the Interaction of Color and Form."
3. Benke, *O'Keeffe*.
4. Linton and Rochon, *Color Model Environments*, 168.
5. Hornung, *Color*.

# Color for Communication

*Colours we use in everyday life tell stories about ourselves.*

—John Hutchings

## Origins of Color Meaning

Color facilitates self-expression and communication. Anthropologist John Hutchings believes that in ancient times humans used color to convey both personal and group identity. By communicating individuality as well as group affiliation, color contributes to the recognizable image of organizations. Color communication is recognized as a core planning criterion when designing (Figure 6-1). By communicating a concept, an image, or a specific brand, color assumes a central role in creating organizational identity.

Undeniably, color messages can be open to interpretation, yet color communication crosses time and place. According to Hutchings, "A large part of [color] usage falls within the area of oral tradition and rituals that have been handed down within families, tribes, or geographical areas. The resulting images are part of our culture;

**Figure 6-1**

Color planning framework guides identity, communication, and associative meaning

they are activities that give us feelings of belonging and of doing the 'right thing.'"[1] Today, color continues to serve as a vehicle for communicating nonverbal messages. Marketing expert Alina Wheeler asserts, "Color can trigger an emotion and evoke a brand association. Distinctive colors need to be chosen carefully, not only to build brand awareness but to express differentiation. Companies such as Kodak and Tiffany's have trademarked their core brand colors."[2] Red, for example, communicates power, aggression, and speed; on center stage in a auto dealership interior, the red of a Lexus signals this message to the consumer while creating an unmistakable focal point (Figure 6-2).

The hues shown in Figure 6-3 illustrate a family of red variations. Darker tonal reds often appear more elegant than a visceral primary red. Some color theorists believe females prefer reds with a bluish cast (such as magenta), while males tend to gravitate toward reds with orange undertones. Color meaning varies according to hue, value, and chroma. Pale pink is associated with fertility and female infants, while young girls in North America tend to associate with more highly saturated pinks in combination with purples.

## Color Symbolism

Archaeological and geological evidence shows that, over 90,000 years ago, humans used ocher in cave paintings for communication.[3] In another study, Hutchings conducted an exhaustive anthropological analysis on color meaning in cross-cultural customs and oral traditions, reviewing an estimated 1,200 folklore documents. He found evidence for economic, social, and historic factors that help explain the origins of color symbolism.

Many cultures associate black and white with rituals and celebrations from death and mourning to weddings and celebrations. From an economic perspective, black and white clothing was less expensive and widely available in earlier times. Not only was black relatively inexpensive, but it also was easier to maintain than other hues. The color associated with mourning in the United States and in many European countries is black, but in China, white represents death. Other cultures incorporate saturated hues into their rituals of mourning. From a sociocultural perspective, death has different meanings around the world. For example, mourners attending funerals in Bali and Mexico often wear brightly colored garments to celebrate the deceased's life, whereas red clothing protects mourners from evil spirits in parts of Africa and the West Indies.

From a historical perspective, color symbolism can reflect landmark events. Hutchings offers the example of how the Finns grew to dislike blue in the 1940s:

**Figure 6-2**

Red Lexus not only creates a visual focal point but also to many communicates speed

**Figure 6-3**

Variations of a single hue communicate distinct messages

"In Finland during World War II, Russian-occupied houses were painted a particular shade of blue. Long after the forces withdrew, this colour could not be used for marketing as it was associated with bad memories of the occupation."[4] Color carries meaning across time and cultures. No single color association is correct. No color association is universal.

Anthropologist David Hunt examines references to color symbolism, particularly in color pairs, in nearly eight hundred examples of folk literature. White/black is the most frequent contrasting pair found in the folk literature studied, and it symbolizes good/bad, day/night, and life/death. Another common color pairing in the literature is red/white, symbolizing potent/neutral and active/passive. When paired with red, white can also symbolize goodness. When red/black are coupled, these hues associate with potency/evil, respectively. Hunt concludes, "The symbolism of colour can be a rather complex subject, partly because some colours have different associations in different contexts."[5] Color symbolism surfaces in the earliest customs and rituals across cultures. Every major hue has both positive and negative meanings.

# Color, Design, and the Market

Research has shown that people associate certain colors with specific building types. In their study, Naz Kaya and Melanie Crosby surveyed 98 college students on such associations.[6] The study found that blue residences appeared "soothing," while red associated with brick façades. Red related to schools and yellow to library interiors and school buses. Institutional buildings such as courthouses associate with gray. For hospitals, blue associated with "blue-colored uniforms" and white communicates hygiene, as in a "white doctor's coat." Red and purple appear most linked with restaurants, shopping malls, and entertainment spaces, including theater and concert halls. Red is stimulating and exciting, while purple conveys a theatrical and creative feeling. White symbolizes a holy color relating to religious buildings. Gray associates with factories, representing maintenance and the color of machinery.

These associations should not prescribe architectural color; rather, the results of the study offer insights into color preconceptions that design clients and occupants might hold. Other research asks this question: How do designers relate color to regional settings rather than adhering to a universal standard? Maria Soledad Dunn interviewed five well-known Ecuadoran architects and designers, who described the color planning process they used in a typical project and talked about how they would employ color in a hypothetical project located in Japan. The designer considered multiple color functions and placed particular significance on sources of vernacular color. One architect cited his source of color inspiration for a particular project as the intense coloration of a ceremonial dress worn by an indigenous tribe. He noted these colors could not be easily transferred to new locations without losing much of their original meaning and cautioned, "I may like the beautiful violet color of the shawls of the Indians from Otavalo, or I may think the deep blue of the Saraguros is beautiful, but there is the risk of doing a superficial conceptualization of color."[7]

Professors Youngsoon Park and Denise Guerin make the case that interior designers may be the best-qualified design professionals to incorporate cultural values into the built environment, and they call on designers to learn about the countries in which their projects are located and to collaborate fully with local professionals and craftspeople.[8] Color symbolism offers a tool for designers to communicate indigenous and vernacular color associations.

A recent study on color and marketing across cultures found differences among consumers.[9] Even associations with blue, a widely popular color, vary somewhat by country. Anglo-Saxon consumers perceive blue products as high-quality, corporate, and masculine. Companies associated with blue include IBM (called Big Blue), Blue Cross Blue Shield, and Tiffany's. In fact, IBM and Tiffany's hold trademarks for their respective organizational blues. The Lanham Act protects trademark color, provided it confers secondary meaning. Some Asian cultures (China, Japan, and South Korea) also associate blue with high-quality and trustworthy products, but in Malaysia, blue associates with cold and evil. Nordic cultures also see blue as cold and masculine; Germans often perceive blue as warm and feminine. While black historically carried meanings of death and lower social rank, it signifies expensive products in Anglo-Saxon and many Asian cultures. Being aware of potential differences in color associations across culture informs color planning.

Color also indicates both the quality and the pricing of a product, and it has been shown to offer the least expensive means of changing public perception of a product. Darker colors usually symbolize high quality; in the United Kingdom, white products are viewed as lower in quality. Beige products carry associations with a more elderly market. Black products appear expensive in the United States and in many Asian countries. Other findings indicate that American consumers associate purple with inexpensive products. Chinese consumers view gray as inexpensive.

Further, color can differentiate within a product line. Companies such as Apple, Gatorade, and Pepsi all created novel colored product lines. Interestingly, transparent or "colorless" product lines, such as Crystal Pepsi, generally have not been well accepted by consumer groups. Highly saturated hues seem to facilitate communication—for example, the Livestrong rubber bracelet is bright yellow.

### *The Meanings of Gray*

Marketing research suggests that gray typically carries negative associations. A recent article in the *New York Times* makes this claim: "Gray has an image problem. Gray is gloomy. Dingy. Depressing. The mid-February complexion of a reclusive aunt. It consistently ranks in the bottom 5 of the 38 colors tracked for consumer preference by the Pantone Color Institute."[10] However, designers effectively work with any color, even one with less than positive associations. Gray is not a uniform hue; grays vary widely in color temperature. In its natural state, cement has a gray-yellow cast, while aluminum has a blue undertone. Grays offer versatility in chromatic as well as neutralized palettes. Architectural colorist Donald Kaufman advocates the versatility of a warm neutral palette, including warm grays. Cooler and darker grays are somewhat harder to integrate into designed spaces. Further, grays can draw attention to the beauty of other colors in the palette. When used alone, gray offers a sophisticated feeling, particularly in combination with white, in light-filled interiors.

# Color Associations Applied

Color associations are most commonly formed with easily recognized hues or values such as red, black, and white. According to Hunt, it is difficult, if not impossible, to create widespread meanings with a complex or tonal color (such as sea green). Wheeler describes the considerations for developing an organizational color message, one that is widely recognized and accepted: "Choosing a color for a new identity requires a core understanding of color theory, a clear vision of how the brand needs to be perceived and differentiated, and an ability to master consistency and meaning over a broad range of mediums."[11] When viewing a logo, individuals first perceive shape and then color, followed by content, such as the name of the organization or the tagline. Color contributes a message, whether in logo and product design or in designed environments. Color can help communicate an organizational message in the following ways:

- *Color and perceived emotionality*—The Gap uses red effectively in its AIDS awareness campaign.

- *Color and perceived innovation*—The color selection of iPods is unique compared to other personal electronics.
- *Color and perceived value*—According to paint manufacturer Benjamin Moore, consumers rated "China white" as more desirable than "chalk white," even though the paints were actually identical.

Consumers generally associate bright, warm colors with low cost and wide accessibility (e.g., McDonald's yellow and red and Home Depot's orange). They typically relate complex and tonal colorations with expense and exclusivity (e.g., Tiffany's trademark blue and Jaguar's sable). Market research has found that organizations associated with blue signify solid, responsible, and financial, while green relates to innovation and caring and yellow communicates young and bright. In the United States, blue most strongly communicates corporate, while in East Asia red is perceived as the preeminent business color. For an organization or a company, "The ultimate goal is to own a color—a color that facilitates recognition and builds brand equity."[12] For example, Tiffany's blue communicates high-end quality, product, and design. The robin's-egg blue is featured prominently in the company's print advertisement, website, packaging design, and marketing campaigns.

Creating consistency across media from print to Web design to product design to interior space requires careful reproduction and execution. The communication of corporate identity and attention to color standardization emerges as the theme of the ensuing project narrative.

## *Corporate Color: Workplace*

Sun Chemical Corporation is the largest producer of printing inks and pigments in the world of packaging and product design. Sun Chemical dyes and pigments introduce color into cosmetics, DVDs, snack food packaging, automotive exteriors, and other applications too numerous to mention. The designers at Gensler were brought in to create Sun Chemical's new headquarters in suburban New Jersey. The design team developed a parsimonious solution that perfectly captures the identity of the company, drawing inspiration for the interior from the color printing systems used by its customer base. The company's customers, regardless of industry, rely on CMYK for color printing and RGB for color imaging.

The workplace floor is planned on a strict module to increase flexibility and accommodate future growth, and it is divided into four nearly identical quadrants. CMYK colors of cyan, magenta, yellow, and black differentiate the four office quad-

rants, each housing a different business unit. An organizational initiative guides each business unit, whose values are illustrated within achromatic murals and representative imagery. The challenge of designing a headquarters for a company in the color business is in striking a balance between a colorful environment and a functional workplace. The CMYK colors are applied in relatively small quantities in tonal work zones that are filled with light and have long views to the outdoors. Sun Chemical's colorful corporate art collection and classic modern furniture enhance the color palette.

The strategic infusion of color from the company logo, Sun Chemical Red (Pantone color PMS 485C) further expresses the corporate identity. This saturated red marks all entrances and transitional spaces with a high-gloss enamel portal (Figure 6-4a).

Dana Jenkins, design principal, emphasizes, "In this project, red became a neutral." Applied liberally throughout the workplace, red underscores the client identity. In some areas, entire walls appear as PMS 485C, while other areas contain bands with the red company logo (Figures 6-4b, c).

A potent example of using color for communication is found in the fourth-floor workplace entry spaces. A square grid of warm colors defines the north entry; an identical grid of cool colors marks the south entry, orienting visitors to the building with color. Lacquered panels in PMS 485C flank a 30-foot timeline illustrating landmark dates and acquisitions in the history of the two-hundred-year-old company. The mural captures the essence of the company by playing with the basic science of the printing process. Large swaths of intersecting color representing CMYK and RGB systems symbolize the lifeblood of Sun Chemical.

Whereas the storyline in Sun Chemical has a clear corporate message that speaks to its identity as defined by its client base, the next case illustrates how a company can reflect regional character in its overall corporate image.

### *Regional Color: Three Resource Centers*

This case centers on issues of communication. The threefold objective facing the designers at Hellmuth, Obata + Kassabaum (HOK) was to capture the essence of the client, reflect regional character, and design sustainably. To create resource centers (or showrooms) for Allsteel and its sister company, Gunlocke, the designers knew they had to build on their client's reputation for reliability and practicality but also demonstrate its most recent innovations in systems furniture. The client, based in Iowa, wanted to strengthen its presence in the Southeast by creating a major resource center in Atlanta, and in short order it planned to open additional resource centers in Boston and Santa Monica.

A key question in this series of projects, according to Karen League, HOK senior vice president and director of interior design in Atlanta, was how to convey regional character: "What is distinctive about each part of the country that contributes to a sense of place and unique locale?" To respond to this question, the Allsteel message was tailored to three geographic contexts. From the beginning, the focus was on regional characteristics that had a wider appeal rather than the respective cities in which the centers were located. Further, all three interiors had to achieve LEED certification, as sustainability was a core value of both the design firm and the client. In the end, color and materiality became critical to telling the story of Allsteel and Gunlocke and contributed to:

- Displaying product lines
- Offering hands-on learning opportunities for architects and designers
- Hosting social events for engaging the design and local business communities

Locating the showrooms in major, centrally located business districts within large urban settings was a strategic move on the part of the company; the intent was to raise the designers' and business leaders' awareness of the manufacturer. A clear sense of corporate identity had to permeate each resource center; this overarching strategy held true from city to city. Of course, the building conditions varied by location: The 12,950-square-foot Atlanta showroom is on the twenty-fourth floor of a newly constructed building; the 9,950-square-foot Boston showroom is on the fourth floor of a historic building; and the 14,000-square-foot Santa Monica center is on the ground floor of an existing building. Across locations, the designers confronted the same challenge: to create an open-plan layout that showcased the product in a proportionally long and narrow space. In addition, each interior had to include a central

space for get-togethers, called the Community Room, complete with a fireplace, ample seating, and tables. This gathering space separated the Allsteel and Gunlocke showrooms and offices.

With these factors kept in mind, color associations reflected contextual appropriateness. For the Southeast, the designers associated the lush, rural landscape with a light tonal green. The central hearth was built with reclaimed stone and surrounded by reconstituted heart pine flooring (see Figures 6-5a–d).

For the Northeast, red symbolizes the historic red glass traditionally produced by area artisans and craftspeople. The central hearth and the slate flooring evoke cobblestone, while custom cherry millwork represents both an indigenous wood and a heritage of furniture making. League summarizes, "This space reflects layers of history and the passage of time" (see Figures 6-6a–c).

For the West Coast, a brighter red introduces a sense of energy. The dominant plaster hearth, weathered wood flooring, and large-scale ceramics embody the casual Californian lifestyle and arts culture (see Figures 6-7a–c).

The interiors provide the context in which the furniture lines are displayed; however, the interiors are subordinate to the product. This is emphasized by League: "The product, the Allsteel and Gunlocke lines, needed to be shown in an interior with carefully adjusted values and saturation. The architectural envelope cannot overwhelm the product. A good balance is needed to engage those in the space."

**Figure 6-5a**

Allsteel/Gunlocke showroom where green symbolizes grassy southern plains (Atlanta)

*Top Left* **Figure 6-5b**
Allsteel hearth and
seating area (Atlanta)

*Top Right* **Figure 6-5d**
Allsteel green training
space (Atlanta)

*Bottom* **Figure 6-5c**
Allsteel showroom
with sample materials
and finishes (Atlanta)

**Figure 6-6c**
Allsteel red training
space (Boston)

*Opposite*
*Top Left* **Figure 6-7a**
Allsteel/Gunlocke
showroom inspired
by Californian
craft tradition
(Santa Monica)

*Top Right* **Figure 6-7b**
Allsteel sample
woods and finishes
(Santa Monica)

*Bottom* **Figure 6-7c**
Allsteel showroom,
Hollywood red
(Santa Monica)

Color Planning for Interiors

Color, lighting, and materials communicate on several levels. Color associations underscore the corporate identity of the client and acknowledge regional uniqueness. The designers created three distinct interiors with the same product lines in similarly configured spaces. The implicit message of sustainability and conservation expresses an organizational value of Allsteel. The design strategy seems to be succeeding; sales have increased, and the client and design firm continue their collaboration with a new showroom project in the Chicago Merchandise Mart.

In the end, Karen League spoke to the significance of color in no uncertain terms:

> Color can be integral to concept development. Beginning with programming criteria, diagramming adjacencies to schematics, the first schematics always begin by addressing color and materials. The concept is client-driven, to develop criteria that are the essence of the client and understood by their stakeholders. The design process needs to unfold in a way that draws the client and stakeholders out in the early visioning sessions and beyond. It is the concept that gives vision form.

The next project narrative tells yet another color story featuring a historically significant building. Working within the parameters of a building marked for the National Register of Historic Places poses distinct challenges. In the case of this corporate headquarters, a thoughtful balance was sought between celebrating the design of a classic mid-century building and creating a contemporary workplace.

## *Mid-century Modern Color: Workplace*

The original building, designed by Skidmore, Owings, and Merrill in 1950, represents the International style. Following this style's emphasis on natural materiality, the original interior spaces incorporated natural materials such as cherry veneer, marble flooring, and local red brick pavers. Some walls featured white laminate and a heavy use of aluminum framing details and reveals (the original occupants of the space manufactured aluminum). Classic furnishings in the lobby included a grouping of LC2 Petit Modèle polished chrome and leather chairs and sofas designed by Le Corbusier and Perriand in 1928.

In the 250,000-square-foot renovation and expansion, spearheaded by AECOM Design, principal Dean Newberry recalls using several strategies to celebrate this historically significant building with five floors of corporate workspaces for nearly five hundred employees and staff (see Figures 6-8a, b).

*Top* **Figure 6-8a**
Fortune 500 company
in International-style
building

*Bottom* **Figure 6-8b**
Lobby space illustrat-
ing truth-in-materials
approach to color

*Color for Communication*     129

This Fortune 500 company had relocated from New York to a southern state and wanted to maintain East Coast sophistication in their new headquarters. The public areas of the building retained the original focus on materiality characteristic of the International style. Many of these public spaces flanked the parklike setting of the inner courtyard.

Cherry veneer walls, marble flooring, window coverings, and furnishings move from the more public areas of the building to the executive office suite. In the CEO's space, the sense of elegant restraint continues with the addition of his authentic leather saddle mounted to create a freestanding focal point (Figure 6-8c). This nod to neutrality extends into executive offices and the formal boardroom by means of cherry, neutral fabrics and finishes, and black leather. Artwork offers significance in the boardroom and throughout the buildings. Large abstract paintings create visual interest in the conference room, while the presentation technology remains hidden.

The workplace also contains areas for informal gatherings and work outside dedicated office spaces. In a room known as the library, employees meet or frequently are seen using laptops individually. Again, the prominent cherry-clad walls direct the palette of 1970s-inspired olive and gold textiles on the upholstered furnishings (Figure 6-8d).

**Figure 6-8d**
Library interior with cherry veneer walls and 1970s-inspired coloration

*Left* **Figure 6-8e**
Monochromatic
gathering space

*Right* **Figure 6-8g**
Salon on subterra-
nean level employs
lighter and brighter
colors than rest of the
building

This coloration extends to other small meeting areas found on each floor of offices. In Figure 6-8e, yellow-greens define the space; a similar space in a different location is blue-green. Other colors relate to the packaging of the company's products. A wide range of corporate colors surfaces in the informal employee dining room (Figure 6-8f). Here, the tonality of the blue-greens, yellow-greens, gold, and purple helps unify both the palette and the space. The subdued coloration relates to the rest of the interior without creating undue contrast.

In the subterranean part of the building, a new coloration emerges in the cluster of small retail shops and service spaces—including a small post office, a large conference center with concierge, a travel agency, an office and print center, a salon, a large fitness center, a cafeteria, a medical clinic with several rooms, and a convenience store selling company products and brands. Much of this level of the facility receives no natural light, thus calling for lighter values and intense colorations. For the salon, the designers wanted a bright environment complementing the clean lines of the interior architecture and specified a light wood in a yellow interior architecture (Figure 6-8g).

The designers created three distinct colorations for the interior: a neutral materiality in the more public and formal spaces, a tonal representation of corporate brands, and palettes of brighter, lighter colors. Each layer of coloration communicates a

distinct message. One palette speaks to an appreciation of mid-century modern design ideals. Another communicates the corporate identity of the organization. A third imparts the distinctive functions of specialty spaces offering a range of amenities. As a whole, the interior reflects the corporate identity and values.

The concluding project in this chapter focuses on a very different type of workplace: an advertising agency. In an agency founded by self-defined mavericks, this office exudes youthful energy and innovation. Again, color offers a tool to communicate the image of the organization as highly creative and cutting-edge. Color communication intersects with color composition in the WestWayne advertising agency, designed by Thompson, Ventulett, Stainback & Associates (tvsdesign).

**Figure 6-8f**
Corporate colors
define cafeteria space

## *Creative Color: Advertising Agency*

It is challenging to design for a client group whose livelihood is pure creativity, but it was exactly this challenge that most excited the design team at TVS. The office space had to capture the essence of WestWayne, self-described as "an independent agency

in thought, mind, and deed. We are independent, both organizationally and in the perspective we bring to the relationships between consumers and brands. We are also a group of professionals who have come from agencies known for their unconventional thinking with a desire to create a place free from the traditional borders so prevalent in conventional advertising."[13] To translate that sentiment into a three-dimensional space, the designers turned to color for the initial wow factor (Figure 6-9a).

From the instant one steps into the tunnel-like space to enter WestWayne, one recognizes the uniqueness of the experience. In this transition space, a seamless curved wall plane arches to connect at midpoint with the ceiling and the edge of the floor. The intense yellow surface reflects its color onto the three adjacent walls, ceiling, and floor surfaces. The entry experience is one of total chromatic immersion (Figure 6-9b).

A high-value but intense hue, such as yellow, maximizes reflected color spilling onto other surfaces (Figure 6-9c). A dark blue would not have reflected nearly as well and might have felt too enclosing and oppressive. The yellow has become a signature for the space, and WestWayne employees mischievously dubbed it the "banana wall."

The sense of playfulness continues as one leaves this compressed entry and enters the airy reception space. The curved yellow tail of the entry wall reaches into the central reception area, offering visual continuity. The reception area prominently features the WestWayne logo, in brushed aluminum, rising from the dark gray accent wall.

In front of the wall, a circle of biomorphic orange and red furniture creates contrast in the primarily achromatic space. Saturated color draws attention to small, collaborative work areas throughout the office. Yet not all the furniture is chromatic. Several sizes of tables and seating appear in white, creating a bridge to the interior architecture. The neutral coloration is enriched by materials and finishes expressing transparency, luster, and sheen in glass, brushed aluminum, and concrete flooring respectively. In the reception space, a large rear projection screen positioned on the wall adjacent to the WestWayne logo displays imagery tailored to visiting clients. This digital show creates a sense of engagement and customization as a messaging tool for the agency.

In other areas of the office, colored lighting is a flexible and dynamic means of energizing the space. A central staircase cuts into the reception area, exposing three levels (Figure 6-9d). The panoramic view from the staircase reveals an airy space, a primarily white interior architecture punctuated with light blues and grays (Figures 6-9e, f). The materials palette emphasizes glass, aluminum, concrete flooring, exposed ductwork, and glossy paint finishes.

The neutral coloration emphasizes openness, and the nearly black stain of the concrete floors contrasts with the lighter interiors. This value creates an illusion of depth in that the distance between floors appears much greater than it actually is

**Figure 6-9c**
WestWayne entrance detail

*Top* **Figure 6-9d**
WestWayne monumental
stairway

*Bottom Left* **Figure 6-9e**
WestWayne large-screen
monitor introduces kinetic
imagery and color into
the space

*Bottom Right* **Figure 6-9f**
WestWayne black-stained
concrete flooring visually
extends the distance
between levels of the
interior

Color Planning for Interiors

from the stairwell. Not only does color communicate imagination and creativity, but it also functions compositionally to:

- Create a sense of compression and spatial release
- Unify and connect the interior spaces
- Enhance the perception of spaciousness
- Develop focal points and areas of emphasis
- Offer flexibility and kinetic imagery

# Summary

Since the beginning of civilization, humans have communicated with color, forming associations with economic, historic, and social origins. These meanings can and do change over time. Earlier in history, male infants were donned in pink, girls in light blue. Today the reverse is true; however, gender-appropriate rules for color are weakening. For product and corporation identity and branding, color remains a powerful tool. Together, color communication and composition contribute to meaningful, well-designed interiors. Expressive color is subjective. Colors are neither inherently good or bad, but their meanings depend both on context and the receiver of the intended message.

## RESEARCH NOTES

In examining the relationship between color associations and building type, Naz Kaya and Melanie Crosby are to be commended for their thoroughness in the research design, as follows:

- Screening the study participants' color vision using the Isihara plate test. This gives confidence in the results of the study, which was based on subjects with normal color vision. Potential participants with impaired color perception were eliminated from the sample.

- Defining color associations in terms of hue, value, and chroma. The color assessment systematically presented hues at three levels of value (light, medium, and low) and saturation (dull, medium, and intense).

The researchers consider all three dimensions of color, creating specificity in the findings. For example, hues associated with residences were lighter and more tonal than the deeper, more saturated colors the sample related to entertainment

*continues*

## RESEARCH NOTES *continued*

spaces. It is important to note that subjects may have wanted to select colors not included in the study, which would influence the results.

The methodology of the study also has limitations:

- The researchers used a convenience sample—that is, they tested college students, who are readily accessible for testing. Therefore, the particular color associations found in the results may be limited to this cohort or age group. Older or younger participants may associate different colors with the building types.

- Similarly, regional bias may arise from the sampling. In two categories of building type (residential and institutional), the participants reported associating red brick with both homes and schools. Brick is a more common building material in some parts of the country than others; therefore, residents in the Southwest, for example, may not report these associations.

- The failure to explicitly differentiate architecture, interior design, and other associations may make it difficult to generalize the findings to other situations. Therefore, some reported associations reference the exterior façade (red brick); others relate to elements in interiors (red theater seats); still others appear completely unrelated to the building type (doctor's uniforms). Teasing out associations between exterior, interior, and components would be informative and should be pursued in future research.

### NOTES

1. Hutchings, "Colour in Folklore and Tradition," 59.
2. Wheeler, *Designing Brand Identity*, 7.
3. Hovers, Ilani, Bar-Yosef, and Vandermeersch, "An Early Case of Color Symbolism."
4. Hutchings, 116.
5. Hunt, "Colour Symbolism in the Folk Literature of the Caucasus," 337.
6. Kaya and Crosby, "Color Associations with Different Building Types."
7. Dunn, *Color Criteria in Cross-cultural Symbolism*, 73.
8. Park and Guerin, "Meaning and Preference of Interior Color Palettes among Four Cultural Groups."
9. Aslam, "Are You Selling the Right Colour?"
10. Pasanella, "Room to Improve," 1.
11. Wheeler, 84.
12. Ibid., 85.

# Color for Engagement

*Color provokes a psychic vibration. Color hides a power still unknown but real, which acts on every part of the human body.*

—Wassily Kandinsky

## The Effects of Color

Attracting. Concealing. Alerting. When brilliantly colored feathers entice a mate, a bird's color marks the beginning of mating season. Camouflage protects an ermine from attack. With a drop in temperature, the fur of the ermine changes from brown to white, so it blends naturally into snowy surroundings. Color signals danger in a poisonous toadstool. These examples from nature only touch the surface of ways color aids a species in survival. Similarly, daily decisions based on color occur almost unconsciously. When grocery shopping, consumers typically pass over blackened or overly green bananas. To drivers, red indisputably signals stop. Color triggers arousal (involuntary) and reaction (voluntary). Color engagement in interior environments

**Figure 7-1**
Color planning
framework examines
responses to color in
a range of settings
and applications

is represented in the color planning framework (Figure 7-1). Examples of how color affects emotion, perceptions of temperature, cognition and memory, flavor and consumption, and even productivity are discussed in the following sections.

## *Arousal and Emotion*

Color triggers innate biological responses: Heart rate increases, breathing quickens, and involuntary perspiration begins. In empirical studies, researchers have found reds to increase emotional and motor responses more than greens and blues. A study of color and emotionality indicated that green elicits the strongest positive emotions of calm, peace, and happiness, but yellow-green associates with disgust and sickness. Some colors evoked both positive and negative emotional reactions; red associated with excitement, happiness, love, and also anger.[1]

## *Color and Temperature*

Color and temperature elicit different psychological and physical responses. Darker paint colors physically absorb more light than lighter colors, slightly affecting the actual temperature of a room. The temperature in two rooms of different colors can be identical, but the temperature in the room painted with warmer colors is perceived as appreciably warmer (6–8°F) than the one painted in cooler hues. All colors can be classified by perceived temperature. Typically, red- and yellow-based colors are thought of as warm, while green-, blue-, and purple-based hues appear cool. It is important to recognize that color temperature also depends on the context.

## *Performance and Memory*

Color can influence learned behavior. For instance, red often signals danger in nature and has been shown to negatively affect test performance. A series of carefully controlled studies found that even brief exposure to red before testing negatively affected performance. The researchers concluded that red is strongly associated with correcting mistakes on papers and tests and, consequently, this hue is intimidating in testing situations. Interestingly, study participants did not appear to be consciously aware they were being influenced by red, but their test performance suffered as a result of the exposure nonetheless. The researchers believe caution should be exercised when red is included in testing situations, and the results "illustrate how color can act as a subtle environmental cue that has important influences on behavior."[2] Sometimes color affects human reactions at a subconscious level and without our knowledge.

Color also affects human memory of events. For example, a recent study showed that colored scenes are remembered more accurately than achromatic ones. In a series of five experiments, investigators compared memory of content in color photographs with that of black and white ones.[3] Regardless of how long they looked at the scenes, the participants remembered the colored images in greater detail than the achromatic ones. Did color have more built-in appeal than black and white images? To further investigate the role of color in human memory, the researchers conducted a related study in which scenes of forests, rocks, and flowers were falsely colored so as not to appear natural. Surprisingly, people did not remember the falsely colored images any better than the achromatic ones. The findings concluded that color in combination with context facilitates the recall of information.

## *Flavor and Consumption*

Cornell food research lab studies relate color to food consumption as well as perception. For example, research participants tended to eat more when presented with a greater variety of color. In the office candy dish, greater quantities of multicolored jelly beans are consumed than those of a solid color.[4]

Another study of taste perception showed that color, more than either quality or price, influenced satisfaction. The same juice was evaluated by consumers in several conditions: The juice was either darkened with food dye (or not), presented in a cup marked with the name of a premium brand (or an inexpensive store brand), or sweetened with sugar (or not). Surprisingly, consumers perceived the greatest taste difference between the juices that were identical except for the dye. The authors concluded, "Our consumers succumbed to the influence of color but were less influenced by the powerful brand and price information."[5]

# Applied Research

Understanding the impact of color on arousal, emotion, and cognitive processes requires careful empirical testing, but assessing the influence of color on performance in designed spaces poses an even greater research challenge. This type of environmentally based research must control for individual differences; environmental consistency, including lighting; and task definition and performance. Researchers must carefully consider the following research variables and issues:

**Individual testing**
- Normal color vision?
- Age and demographics?
- Tolerance for environmental stimulation?

**Environmental setting**
- Rationale for color selection?
- Characteristics of settings assessed?
- Lighting?

**Person-environment connection**
- Time spent in interior?
- Tasks performed?
- Outcomes measured?
- Real-world relevance?

One such study examined work productivity in relation to three office color conditions. To her credit, Nancy Kwallek and her colleagues controlled many variables in this empirical examination of workplace productivity.[6] First, the research team screened the participants on color vision using color plate tests. After testing, the sample was divided into those considered "high screeners," who were least affected by environmental conditions, "low screeners," who were more sensitive and distractible, and another group of those who showed a moderate ability to screen information. Productivity was defined by the researchers as the performance level for basic clerical tasks in white, red, and green offices with identical lighting and design.

Productivity was measured over a four-day period. Findings did not show clear patterns of behavior related to office color. Yet one interesting finding was that both the high and low screeners initially appeared distracted by the red interior, but over time all participants seemed to grow accustomed to this hue. In other cases, environmental color can make occupants increasingly agitated with prolonged exposure. Office color and productivity may be subject to the Hawthorne effect, whereby employees simply like what they have control over changing. If this is true, productivity may be increased by asking employees to select their individual office colors (when they have individual offices) with the option to change hues every few years.

# Consumer Experiences, Services, and Health

The question of how color influences behavior in interiors does not lend itself to easy answers. Color perceptions change according to lighting variations, spatial configuration of the interior, primary tasks occurring in the space, and differences among the people using the space. Color also is affected by materials, textures, and patterns in the interior environment. Color effects may attenuate or strengthen with the passage of time. Individual and age differences in color acuity exist. However, color guidelines *can* improve environments where humans spend the majority of their time.

Color, for example, helps create a residential atmosphere within an institutional hospital setting. General consensus exists on eliminating "hospital white" and "hospital green." Environmental color specialists Frank Mahnke and Rudolf Mahnke argue that a predominately white, brightly lit interior environment contributes to eye fatigue and psychological discomfort.[7] In settings dominated by hard surfaces, white does not enhance sensory variety. It is not difficult to identify human needs and problems related to color use in settings with little tactile stimulation, but posing effective alternatives is. Color findings derived from empirical research may be hard to generalize in actual living spaces. Color formulas cannot address variations in illumination, materials, and the design of architectural space. However, criteria on the behavioral objectives for color can guide decision making.

*Opposite*
**Figure 7-2a**
Lotte Avenue L
specialty store is
designed to increase
consumer buying
(Seoul)

Environmental color, for example, can reinforce or counter the effects of age-related decrements in color vision. Older adults have trouble discriminating between blues and greens; thus, creating color contrast with other hues is essential. This approach serves a practical as well as an aesthetic purpose in highlighting potential environmental hazards—for example, on staircases, where treads and risers must be clearly delineated. Karen Carpman and Myron Grant suggest that in environments for elderly users, color can be used to organize a series of rooms so they appear to be grouped in some way; it can signify change, suggest outlines or emphasize contours, signal an alert, or work as a background surface on which a focal object can be easily distinguished. It can also camouflage certain areas.[8]

In normal aging, the lens of the human eye yellows, hardens, and scatters more light. Typically, older adults need reading glasses to see near distances and are more sensitive to glare. Color vision remains fairly normal, but the lens (cornea) of the eye gradually yellows. These changes result in shifts in color perception. Blues and greens appear more similar; blues look darker, and purples appear more like reds. Night vision decreases as the rods receive less light, which also results in more scattering of light and reduced luminance sensitivity.

The following project narratives describe the ways designers use color to positively impact the people who occupy their spaces. In the first cases, color is designed to support an enjoyable shopping experience and, of course, to increase sales. The next example of color and behavior succinctly describes how color creates ambiance in a spa. Most importantly, the chapter ends by focusing on healthcare settings, where color, lighting, and materials play an instrumental role in the design of a neonatal intensive care unit and a pediatric clinic.

*Page 146*
*Top Left* **Figure 7-2b**
Lotte Avenue L shows
color change defining
planes and thresholds
in retail spaces

*Top Right* **Figure 7-2c**
Lotte Avenue L
color and form lead
shoppers through
the interior

*Bottom* **Figure 7-2d**
Lotte Avenue L
contains a white
square plane that
reflects onto the
flooring

## Understated Color: Korean Luxury Shopping

This project describes a high-end retail establishment in Seoul, South Korea. Designed to be spectacular, the design concept for the setting is an interior garden with a wall of flowers (Figures 7-2a–c). The repetition of flowers against the understated granite wall creates a neutral but opulent backdrop. From season to season, year to year, the merchandise changes, but the interior architecture was designed for permanence.

Recent marketing research differentiates recreational from task-oriented consumers. The recreational shopper enjoys the process of shopping, whereas the task-oriented consumer is focused and intentional in his or her activities. From the designers' perspective, the typical consumers in this location would probably be more recreational in their orientation, so the interiors are designed to support longer, more leisurely shopping excursions.

Some consumer research recommends designing chromatic, highly stimulating physical environments for the recreational shopper. However, such shoppers may differ depending on the market segment and culture. From their experience in South Korea, the design team noted that, in general, these consumers view shopping in recreational terms, particularly in the luxury sector. The tonal, sophisticated interior architecture that appears successful in this design contains flowing interiors and curvilinear pathways that seem to pull consumers through the space (Figures 7-2c–e), ending in private destinations (Figure 7-2f). Curving pathways create a sense of mystery and allure in the environment.

## *Gourmet Color: Korean Specialty Market*

Creating distinctive consumer experiences for varied market demographics requires thoughtful color planning. The next cases describe how the Pavlik Design Team (PDT) approached two distinct retail experiences. The first case is a gourmet marketplace designed to invite a leisurely shopping experience; the second is a big-box grocery that offers a broad selection of affordable products to a wide customer base. Both concept-driven designs stem from similar creative processes, but the results are very different. Fernando Castillo, senior project director at the PDT, and his colleague, Amy Roesler, an experienced color and materials specialist with the firm, describe the projects.

*Left* **Figure 7-2e**
Lotte Avenue L contains saturated red acting as a focal point

*Right* **Figure 7-2f**
Lotte Avenue L illustrates light-dark contrast in a private viewing area

*Above* **Figure 7-3a**
Galleria Gourmet
Emporium is defined
by light-dark contrast
(Seoul)

*Below* **Figure 7-3b**
Galleria Gourmet
Emporium empha-
sizes coloration in
materiality

The PDT developed the client branding and design for the Gourmet Emporium, which aimed for a luxury-oriented, European type of retail experience. The project setting was in Seoul, South Korea, and the target consumer group was the 30–40-year-old, upper-income demographic that embraced the latest trends, was brand-conscious, and traveled widely. For this design, the Pavlik team developed a metaphorical concept: food as art. No accent wall hues were introduced into the space; the food products and packaging became areas of emphasis. Value contrasts of light and dark contribute to a fashion-forward atmosphere. On central columns, food and produce thematic art pieces are displayed, while signage, in overscale gilded frames, again references the food-as-art concept.

The Gourmet Emporium represents more than food; it is a destination and an experience (Figures 7-3a–c). The layout of the interior is meant to direct consumers through a simple loop and preserve open sightlines. This spatial configuration enables customers to discover the latest specialty foods, eat at the sushi bar, or have a juice or gourmet coffee at the beverage counter. The space is designed to produce a pleasant, leisurely experience. Shopping behavior in Seoul can be described as intensely social; it is not uncommon to see groups shopping together and socializing in boutiques during an excursion that lasts the greater part of a day. Armed with this knowledge, the designers set out to engage consumers with products and encourage them to spend time and maximize purchases in an elegant interior.

A fairly neutral palette of materials reinforces specialized zones within the 30,000-square-foot space: deli, bakery, organic produce section, specialty meat and seafood areas, dry goods section (with a large selection of specialty teas and coffees), wine area, florist, and spaces for eating and, of course, purchasing. Each zone is defined by a unique textural element; for example, the deli features a Jerusalem stone wall veneer. Custom display cases in dark brown with an aluminum finish create a sophisticated, elegant look. The inspiration for these display fixtures stemmed from a recent line of contemporary residential furnishings by Pucci.

**Figure 7-3c**
Galleria Gourmet Emporium showcases the products within a neutral interior envelope

One challenge was the location and proportion of the existing space. The Emporium is housed on the basement level of nine floors of retail space. To create continuity with boutique spaces such as Prada and Armani, the Pavlik team employed a similar design vocabulary in the Gourmet Emporium. Actually, at one point in their process, the designers imagined how Armani might have designed the interior. On the whole, the palette is neutral, with white crystalline glass flooring repeated from the upper retail floors. To confront the long and narrow space, the designers introduced more character in the ceiling through tresses and soffits, again corresponding to the retail zones.

Another issue involved lighting the windowless space. Typically, grocers employ overhead fluorescent lights for overall ambient lighting; however, the designers decided to model the space after a high-end boutique with specialty lighting. "Compared with the 60 to 80 foot-candles found in typical U.S. supermarkets, the Gourmet Emporium checks in at a mood-enhancing 30 to 60 foot-candles." The primary light source is ceramic metal halide in low wattages; this yields strong color rendition and conserves energy, compared to incandescent sources. This type of lamp also does not subject the perishable products to temperature extremes.

Pragmatic issues surface even in high-end interiors, and the Gourmet Emporium was no exception. Composite wall surfaces (rather than wood veneers) were required in the meat and fish department for easy maintenance and to uphold health and hygiene standards.

## Big-Box Color: Mexican Grocery

In contrast to the upscale gourmet venue, PDT designed a 100,000-square-foot big-box renovation project in Monterrey (Figures 7-4a, b). The existing space was poorly organized and did not adequately display the products. The intent for the renovation was to clearly demarcate product zones and circulation pathways with strong accent color, bold graphics, and signage. For this project, color and super graphics energized the space, according to Castillo. "Color offered the most cost-effective solution for maximum impact." The environment was designed to stimulate the senses—the smell of fresh bread baking permeated the space at all times.

The designers, color and design specialists, and graphics team worked closely to create a fully "sensual" interior. Ceiling soffits echo the curving line in the vinyl tile flooring; color contrast defines the primary paths of circulation and café areas. Color, materiality, and furniture selection encourage shoppers to stop for a quick bite but not spend too much time in the area (Figure 7-4c). In the café space, specified chairs are not comfortable to sit in for long. In Mexico, as in South Korea, retail, even grocery shopping, is a social experience.

The design of this store served as a prototype for the retail chain. Castillo, who was involved in both projects, says the Mexican culture is more accepting of saturated color, and brightly colored mosaics will be increasingly incorporated into the newest stores. However, there is not only a cultural difference but a price point difference where research on color psychology indicates that saturated colors, such as orange, declassify products, while darker and more neutralized hues create more expensive associations. While this has not been empirically quantified, the success of the grocery store is abundantly clear. The stock in the retailer rose significantly after the renovation, and the client reported a highly positive consumer response to the space. Again, color contributed to the design objective of creating an environment in which to shop with increased efficiency, purchase large quantities, and generate a high volume of sales.

Opposite

Top **Figure 7-4a**
Mega Cuernavaca
Supermarket
illustrates hue contrast
(Monterrey, Mexico)

Bottom **Figure 7-4b**
Mega Cuernavaca
contains color signage
and graphics that
indicate circulation
patterns

*Opposite*
**Figure 7-4c**
Mega Cuernavaca
café signals quick and
affordable dining

*Above* **Figure 7-5a**
The spa at Ponte
Vedra Inn and Club
creates a relaxing
environment
(Ponte Vedra, Florida)

*Left* **Figure 7-5b**
The spa features
natural materials
such as rough-hewn
stone and wood

*Right* **Figure 7-5c**
The spa incorporates
innovative materials
such as glass panels
with reedlike qualities

## *Calming Color: Spa*

This contemporary interior is designed to integrate Asian, European, and local elements in a chic spa in Florida. To create a sense of calm and rejuvenation, the architectural color is monochromatic and defined by natural materials, accented with a light tonal green (Figures 7-5a–c). This coloration extends from the more public areas of the interior to the treatment rooms, which feature cream limestone, travertine, Irish granite, and green marble. In the spa, color appears delicate and the natural textures varied. The designers from the Pavlik Design Team focused on light and dark contrast (instead of introducing contrasting hues or saturation levels). The gender-designated areas are quite similar in feel, but the spaces designed exclusively for men contain darker values than do the interiors for women. Color and materiality in the spa's retail space are somewhat more vibrant, yet they maintain the feeling of relaxation.

## *Healing Color: Neonatal Intensive Care Unit*

Optimizing health and healing drove decisions about color, lighting, and materials in this neonatal intensive care unit (NICU). This case is noteworthy for the close collaboration of designers and medical staff in considering ways to support premature infants and their mothers and other family members as well as NICU staff. Initiating a benchmarking process, the medical director at Shands Hospital NICU sponsored a small group of medical staff and designers from Flad Architects to visit select NICUs in Ohio, Georgia, and Florida. This firsthand experience offered a frame of reference to begin the 9,000-square-foot Shands renovation. The benchmarking process led to the decision that the layout of the space had to give staff direct visual access and close proximity to their tiny patients, yet allow some privacy for bonding between mothers (and families) and their babies.

The renovation consisted of twenty-two patient areas, a waiting room, two examination rooms, two extra-corporeal membrane oxygen (ECMO) treatment rooms, and two spaces in which to perform surgery. In the surgical area, a removable divider offers the flexibility to create a larger area for performing complicated procedures requiring up to fifteen medical staff members.

Within the NICU, mothers and families frequently spend large quantities of time with the infants, often six hours and more each day, confronting the many stresses of a baby born before full term. Likewise, the NICU staff works under emotionally strained conditions. A comfortable, relaxing, and appealing environment is needed. Maria-Luisa Riviere, lead project designer, recalls discussions with the staff about their vision for the space. The staff made a strong case for increasing the natural lighting in the unit. Riviere responded by increasing the number of windows and creating a large circular skylight in the waiting area. Further, a staff member mentioned that time in nature helped reduce tension. This directed Riviere to the idea of using curving shapes and tonal greens and blues. Not only do these shapes elicit a feeling of nature, but also the staff voiced preference for rounded edges (as at a

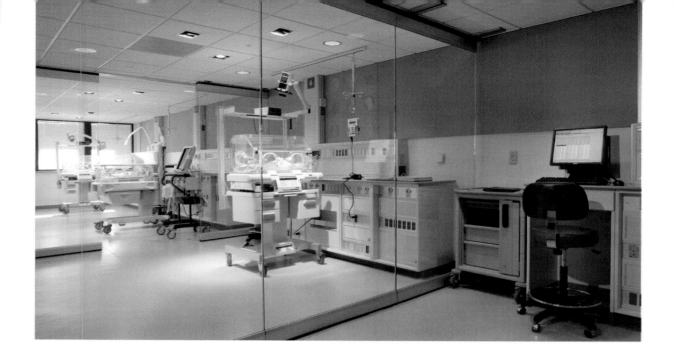

**Figure 7-6a**

Neonatal intensive
care unit (NICU) at
Shands Hospital incor-
porates limited color
(Gainesville, Florida)

moment's notice they might have to move quickly across the space and do not want
to encounter sharp corners).

The staff expressed additional needs. For example, they wanted a greater number
of emergency outlets than are required by building code (these are powered by
generators in case of power outages). These emergency outlets, color-coded red, are
found throughout the space. Other pragmatics drove color decisions in planning
the NICU.

To minimize the disruption of materials upkeep and replacement, the coloration
had to be limited in this critical care unit, so Riviere focused on the concept of blue
water, reinforced by form and materiality. She selected a light tonal blue from one
of Shands' approved standards; in hospitals, such regulations ensure consistency and
ease of maintenance. This blue relates to other areas in the hospital, and the specified
blue paint and fabric can be easily replaced when needed (Figure 7-6a). Psychologically, blue is calming and is often cited as the most widely preferred color. More criti-
cally, a neutralized or high-key coloration would not influence an accurate reading of
the infants' skin color—an indicator of health—by medical staff members.

Riviere carefully considered where to apply the blue in the space. She decided
to incorporate an accent of blue on the ceiling plane, forming a curvilinear ribbon
that pulls attention up and away from the vast array of medical equipment (Figure
7-6b). Dropping a 4-inch curving soffit creates the illusion of a higher ceiling; the

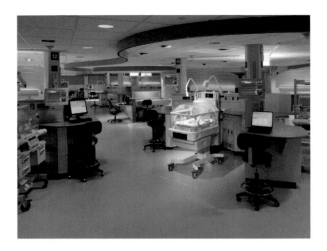
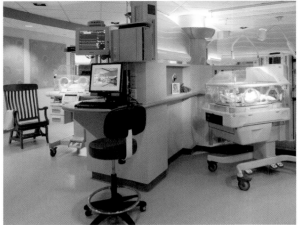
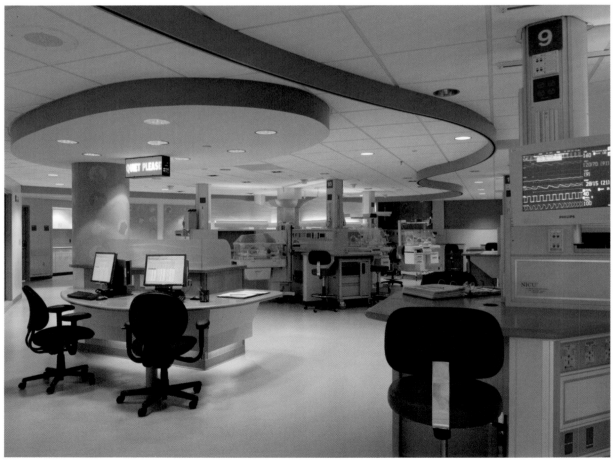

renovation conditions would not permit raising the existing 8-foot ceiling height. In addition to creating a more pleasing space, the blue soffit also reinforces the circulation pattern around the perimeter patient areas. The headwalls, which separate four patient areas in a pinwheel layout, contain translucent glass panels, illuminated with a soft blue light (Figure 7-6c). These panels offer both visual access and privacy while reinforcing the feeling of water both through color and an etched wave pattern. This pattern appears more prominent at night because of the indirect lighting from the glass.

Properly specified lighting promotes infant well-being; therefore, lighting considerations became more critical than color decisions in this project. Reinforcing the infants' circadian rhythm is critical to supporting their development and growth. Therefore, low lighting encourages infants to sleep at night, but illumination is still needed for the staff to perform their duties (Figure 7-6d). The staff can control all incandescent lights with dimmer switches. Importantly, the designers specified lighting for the NICU to address the following:

- *Examinations and medical procedures*—high-intensity directional lighting
- *Circulation*—recessed lighting on the ceiling for navigation and low-level floor lighting installed under cabinetry for easy movement at night
- *Privacy*—indirect lighting on the translucent panels
- *Ambiance*—indirect lighting on the central columns
- *Well-being*—natural lighting from windows and skylights

In addition to lighting, noise levels must be controlled, as premature infants are extremely sensitive to sound; the point is so important that two fixtures, installed in the ceiling, flash "Please quiet" when optimal sound levels are exceeded. Fabric panels help with the acoustics and introduce a light blue into the operating space, while a high-key abstract pattern covers several columns. The rubber flooring, in a light tonal blue, helps with sound control as well as maintenance. The flooring also helps support staff members, who may stand for long periods.

The layout of the NICU moved from a linear station arrangement to a group of semiprivate areas designed for a more holistic approach to infants and families. At the ribbon-cutting ceremony, families who had spent time in this unit at Shands before the renovation marveled at the transformation. Several years later, Riviere reports, the staff continues to be pleased with the unit, especially citing the increased natural lighting. She attributes this to "the high level of staff participation, involvement, and ownership in the process, [which] created strong satisfaction with the NICU."

*Opposite*

*Top Left* **Figure 7-6b** NICU introduces a tonal blue band into the ceiling soffit for visual relief

*Top Right* **Figure 7-6c** NICU separates the infant areas with a partition of frosted glass illuminated in blue

*Bottom* **Figure 7-6d** NICU staff and families need to move easily through the interior under low lighting levels

**Figure 7-7a**

Affinity Pediatric
Healthcare Facility
(Central Wisconsin)

## Wellness Color: Pediatric Clinic

The client for this project, Affinity Health System (AHS), is a leading healthcare provider in the Midwest. The community-based clinic project shows the central role of color and materials in creating pediatric spaces. The color planning process for AHS recognized the unique needs of the adolescents, children, and their families seeking care as well as the staff working in the clinic. The design team at Flad Architects in Madison, Wisconsin, had worked with AHS in developing a clinic prototype for the Midwest region that had scored high marks from patients, families, and medical staff. For the pediatric clinic, the design strategy was to adapt this well-accepted prototype for younger patients, their families, and staff. The overall plan for the 12,000-square-foot facility would incorporate essentially the same spatial organization and materials as other AHS clinics, but colors, finishes, furnishings, and artwork would be tailored to a new population of users. Further expectations were to achieve LEED certification and to communicate the organizational identity of AHS.

One issue that surfaced quickly was patient demographics. Pediatric clinics serve newborns, children, and teenagers through age 18, though 75 percent of the patients are under age 15. This challenged the designers to develop an environment that is inviting for older children and teenagers as well as the youngest patients.

Ideas for the project concept surfaced during visioning sessions with the medical staff, who wanted the space to be associated with nature, and the clinic even includes a patient-oriented garden designed to promote well-being. Located in a natural setting, the building site is close to a river (Figure 7-7a). The designers listened carefully to their client group but veered from translating these concepts too literally; there were to be no fish-shaped children's chairs or large boat structures in the play areas, for example. A thematic approach risked alienating the older patients and did not align with the architecture. Further, the art program did not incorporate realistic subject matter but rather consisted of non-objective or abstracted artwork offering color, texture, and form. The designers were able to reference the natural environment in subtle ways that complement the contemporary quality of the architecture and are acceptable in the Wisconsin market.

People entering the space encounter a vaulted, wood-paneled ceiling, a curtain wall of glass, natural stone, and a freestanding aquarium. Patients check in at a large custom-built maple reception desk (Figure 7-7b). Immediately, the interior design accommodates different age groups of patients and their families with clear color and materials designations. In the entry space, the family members and patients can opt to wait in one of the clearly demarcated waiting areas. This attention to the type

of patient is intended to reduce patient anxiety. Not only the colors but also the materials and finishes reinforce this effort. For teenagers, a neutralized area allows privacy and offers space to use a laptop or read; for younger children, curved colored planes suspended from the ceiling visually identify a dedicated, sheltered play area with smaller-scale furnishings (Figure 7-7c). Yet another zone contains an enormous curving sofa with built-in table surfaces that offer flexibility in seating. For instance, a mother with an infant in a carrier accompanied by other children and adults could comfortably wait in this area.

The designers specified lighter woods, such as maple, for the reception desk and other millwork, gray work surfaces, and a stained pine paneling to define the ceiling treatment. This lighter wood conveys a more informal and contemporary feeling than did the formal, traditional cherry tones used in the majority of AHS clinics. All

**Figure 7-7b**
Pediatric reception space organizes the large interior through color and form

*ich as these that the kingdom of God belongs."*

**Figure 7-7c**

Pediatric reception
facility incorporates
suspended color
elements to define
a play area

clinics use the standard eggshell wall color seen in the lobby, but the wall color in the examination rooms and adjacent hallways differs markedly. Varied in hue, the color palette here is more highly saturated. In the hallway outside the exam rooms, projecting doorframes of yellow, blue-purple, and green identify specific exam rooms for patients and family members. These more saturated colors exude a youthful quality, but the designers deliberately did not juxtapose them to control the level of contrast in the space (Figure 7-7d).

The staff, instrumental in the color planning process, warned the designers not to use saturated hues that influence skin tone, creating a colored cast on patients' complexions. In the end, the designer specified an accent wall at the end of the exam room that was flanked by off-white walls. This facilitates patient diagnosis while creating an inviting comfort level for patients. Further, the involved staff believed red was not an appropriate color for the exam rooms, given its association with blood. Yet the clients supported the idea of introducing red in smaller quantities on benches and stools and related the space to the red AHS logo.

In refining the palette, the designers carefully considered the value and saturation levels of the paint colors for the examination rooms. Initially, they proposed a scheme of green, blues, and yellows that were acceptable to the client, but on closer review the value level of the green and blues had to be lightened. The designers then adjusted the palette so the value of the wall color was in the same range as the flooring. A darker band of the hue was introduced in the room, helping create a more intimate space. Again, colors shifted from being the primary accent wall color to appearing as a more contained accent band or furniture element. The designers were careful not to specify primary colors that would seem too childish for some patients. The wave elements suspended from the ceiling are not a primary triad, for example, but incorporate more complex blues with purple and green undertones.

The color planning for this project was designed from the floor up. The coloration of the carpeting is markedly different than the traditional greens and purples found in many healthcare facilities. The carpet tile offers multiple patterns that can be combined in a variety of ways for zoning and marking circulation paths. The entry space in the clinic uses a large pattern that project designer Jennifer Kauls compares to worn jeans, a coloration offering an almost universal ability to coordinate well with other hues and patterns. The transition spaces employ a yellow pattern and then move into a smaller-scale pattern of the jean color in the examination corridor.

**Figure 7-7d**
Hallway defines room use by color

A variation of the blue-jean carpeting is installed in the staff area, which has dedicated workspaces for nurses, doctors, and other employees. In this back-of-the-house area, the carpeting contains only textural variation, without pattern, to create a calm, sophisticated feeling that distinguishes the staff zone from patient areas (Figures 7-7e, f). The designers specified carpet with recycled content, 100 percent recyclable fabrics, zero-VOC paints, and sheet vinyl in the examination rooms. Vinyl is not a

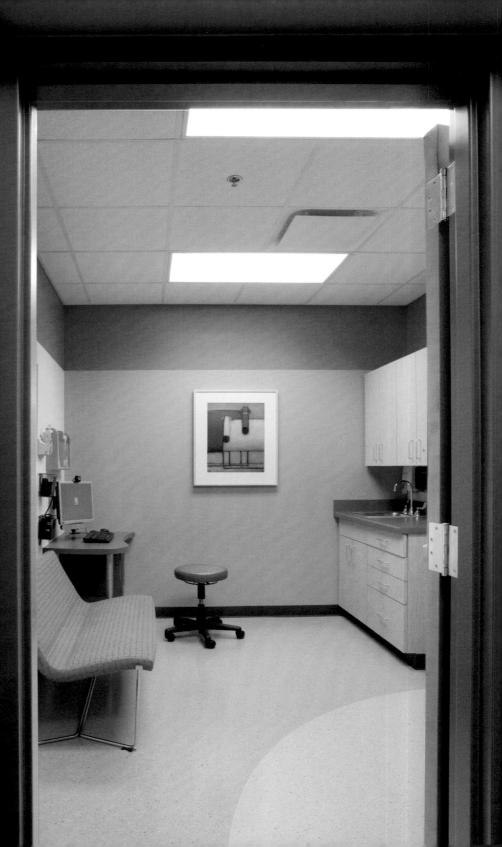

Exam
Room 5

*Opposite* **Figure 7-7e**
Exam rooms continue
the color scheme but
have neutral side walls
to facilitate accurate
diagnosis and gauging
of skin tone

*Above* **Figure 7-7f**
The nursing station
has flooring similar to
the rest of the facility
but in colors specific
to this space restricted
to employees

sustainable material but was selected for its ease of maintenance (including minimal chemicals required for cleaning).

Kauls believes color and finishes became essential elements of the welcoming environment for young patients and their families. She maintains color creates the greatest impact in the reception areas and exam rooms. Here, color and finishes create distinct zones of activities, orient individuals to their destinations in the clinic, and convey a caring and patient-centered attitude. Not limited to the first-impression reception area, this quality extends into the most private and frequently neglected patient exam rooms.

The only aspect of the color Kauls would revisit, if given the opportunity to do so, is the amount used in some parts of the interior. For example, the coloration in the examination hallway and rooms proved very successful, and extending this palette into the eggshell-painted interior spaces, from the designer's perspective, would create an even more engaging experience. Most satisfying is the design's sense of timelessness. Whereas the typical renovation cycle for healthcare facilities is seven to ten years, Jennifer Kauls proudly predicts the neutrality of the glass, wood, stone, gray work surfaces, and carefully selected color scheme in the AHS pediatric clinic should last well beyond a decade.

# Summary

Exposure to color produces real physiological, psychological, and behavioral responses. Empirical findings on color and emotion, temperature, memory, and the perception of flavors and even food and beverage consumption and preference shed light on the influence of color. More complex behaviors, like workplace performance, are much more difficult to research and predict. Learning from project narratives set in a variety of contexts suggests ways in which color, lighting, and materiality may affect the quality of experience in an interior space and even the health of its occupants. Influencing unconscious thoughts and conscious decisions, the impact of color on the human response is undeniable.

# RESEARCH NOTES

## Research on Test Performance

Andrew Elliot and his collaborators carefully controlled the red samples used in this study.[9] Using the Munsell system, the reds were controlled for hue, brightness (value), and saturation (chroma). A spectrophotometer measured the exact color swatches, and a high-quality printer generated the color samples used for testing. Researchers who want to replicate and expand this study need exact information on the testing materials and how the color dimensions were controlled.

## Research on Workplace Productivity

A meta-analysis of over two hundred color studies concluded that research examining the relationship between environmental color and human performance has proven contradictory or inconclusive.[10] Research flaws often include the following factors:

- Lack of necessary experimental controls and design measures
- Poor experimental room settings for testing
- Inadequate measures of productivity and other appropriate outcome measures
- Lack of long-term assessment

**NOTES**

1. Kaya and Epps, "Relationship Between Color and Emotion."
2. Elliot, Maier, Moller, Friedman, and Meinhardt, "Color and Psychological Functioning," 164.
3. Wichmann, Sharpe, and Gegenfurtner, "The Contributions of Color to Recognition Memory for Natural Sciences."
4. Kahn and Wansink, "The Influence of Assortment Structure on Perceived Variety and Consumption Quantities."
5. Hoegg and Alba, "Taste Perception: More Than Meets the Tongue."
6. Kwallek, Soon, and Lewis, "Workweek Productivity, Visual Complexity, and Individual Environmental Sensitivity in Three Offices of Different Color Interiors."
7. Mahnke and Mahnke, Color and Light in Man-made Environments.
8. Carpman and Grant, Design That Cares.
9. Elliot, Maier, Moller, Friedman, and Meinhardt.
10. Beach, Wise, and Wise, The Human Factors of Color in Environmental Decisions.

# 8

# Color for Pragmatics

*Color and texture are inseparable. In fact, the same colors and materials change character depending on their surface treatment and finish.*

—Jean-Philippe Lenclos and Dominique Lenclos

The pragmatics of color emphasize the functional side of color planning, where decisions about color reflect practical realities (Figure 8-1). Pragmatics relate to economics, material properties, design constraints, or renovation workarounds in a design project. For example, the budget allocation for an interior space may necessitate paint instead of other materials or finishes (Figure 8-2). Color selections also can be limited within a systems furniture line. In another example, a designer may decide to retain existing terrazzo flooring in a renovation, influencing the direction of the project's color palette. Further, sustainable performance expectations for materials and finishes affect coloration. If energy savings is a project priority, a lighter wall color may be specified because its reflectivity results in fewer coats of paint for coverage than darker values. Ultimately, the interior will require less interior lighting than if

167

dark paints were specified. Another practical reality surfaces when selecting flooring for high-traffic spaces in commercial interiors; this usually means medium-value, textured carpeting to support maintenance and longevity. Importantly, a commitment to sustainable design means a commitment to pragmatic color decision making as part of a holistic design process.

# Not-So-Big House

Annually for nearly two decades, *Life* magazine has invited well-known designers to create an ideal residence for the American family. The year the firm SALA spearheaded this challenge, the design team, including architect Sarah Susanka, designed two versions of a 2,100-square-foot home: the Back to Basics and the Whole Nine Yards. Each prototype demonstrates principles of good design at different price points. Color, whether through paint or materials, is central to the quality of the space.

In Susanka's words:

Whereas expensive finishes were avoided in the Back to Basics house, in favor of [paint] color, here [Whole Nine Yards] materials such as wood and stone have

been employed to give the home warmth. When budget constraints are less of an issue, such natural materials add a timeless quality and character to a house. But they're not critical to livability or personality; their effect is simply different.[1]

In the Back to Basics dream house, paint color offers an economical way to add character to the interior architecture. From a practical standpoint, color provides maximum impact for minimal cost. One example shows how Back to Basics uses color pragmatically: Here, a wall-mounted, custom buffet creates greater visual impact due to color. This contemporary buffet uses a limited amount of wood cabinetry, but a strategically planned wall color surrounding it makes the unit appear much more substantial. The wall color closely complements that of the wood, creating the illusion that the buffet extends from floor to ceiling. Reinforcing this effect, a contrasting yellow-green tint is painted on the adjacent ceiling, and a dropped soffit over the buffet frames the similar hues of the wood and the wall.

The Back to Basics prototype introduces a palette of limited hues that varies in amount from space to space within the interior. The terra cotta in a relatively large space becomes an accent in another. Again and again, Back to Basics illustrates a visual language for integrating pragmatics with the shaping of form. Color makes a sizable contribution to the small, captivating homes Susanka so passionately advocates.

# Origins of Color Pragmatics

Historically, opportunities for uniqueness in exterior color were often restricted by the accessibility of materials. Limited means of transportation resulted in towns and villages built with materials from the area. Today, sustainable practices encourage the use of local and regional materials. Some provinces and even small countries continue to maintain strict building codes regulating exterior color.[2, 3] Planned communities across the United States often regulate the coloration of commercial and residential building façades. Pragmatic reasons for using color sometimes can be surprising, as in the following investigation of a striking blue kitchen in St. Croix. This section was researched and written by Tiffany Lang for this book.

### *Color Origins: Blue Kitchens around the World*
Museum patrons are pleasantly surprised to see the vibrant blue kitchen in the Lawaetz Family Museum located in St. Croix, U.S. Virgin Islands, in the Caribbean.

Currently a museum, this building was part of a sugar plantation in the 1750s. The estate was purchased by Carl Lawaetz in 1896 to be used as a cattle ranch and has been in the Lawaetz family since that time. The kitchen itself was built in 1909 to replace an earlier unattached kitchen. Docent Irene Lawaetz tells visitors that the walls of the kitchen are painted blue because of a European belief that blue repels flies. According to Lawaetz, this particular treatment consists of a water-based mixture that includes lime and blue pigment.[4]

A similar hue is found in Leslie Geddes-Brown's kitchen in Suffolk, England. It is painted in a blue that has been limewashed. Geddes-Brown notes, "Our inspiration was the eighteenth-century kitchen at Calke Abbey [located in England], which was painted almost exactly this strong blue. Apparently, this colour was used in many kitchens and on French shutters to deter flies, but I later discovered it was the scent of the herb used in the early dye and not the actual colour which put off the flies."[5]

Another blue kitchen, part of a property called Gonzola in Italy, is painted in Tuscan peasant colors. "The walls of the kitchen have been painted with a stunning blue chalk wash which is characteristic of the old kitchens in Tuscan peasant houses as blue was renowned to keep the flies away from food in summer."[6]

How prevalent was this belief in the insect-repelling power of blue paint? These and other examples indicate this belief may have been widespread at the time. A prime example is the prototype for the Frankfurt Kitchen, which was painted in blue. This kitchen was designed by Margarete Schutte Lihotzky in Frankfurt, Germany, in 1926. It is considered the precedent for modern built-in kitchens. David Ryan, a curator at the Minneapolis Institute of Arts, where one of these kitchens is installed, makes this comment in an article: "The Germans were very obsessed with hygiene, and this design was a new way to exist in a kitchen." Pointing out the pest-resistant aluminum bins for flour, sugar, and other supplies, he notes, "Even the color was hygienic because studies then indicated that the color blue repelled flies."[7]

One account describes the process and materials used in treating walls in Victorian kitchens:

How did the Victorians decorate the walls of their kitchens? Kitchen walls were of plain plaster, regularly whitewashed or distempered. A bag of laundry blue in the paint bucket imparted a faint blue tinge to the walls, which was said to repel flies and imparted a feeling of coolness to the room. Lower down, the walls were covered with a high dado of tongue-and-groove boarding painted with washable gloss paint, tiles or glazed brick for hard wear and hygiene.[8]

The "laundry blue" referred to in this passage is a laundry whitener introduced in the 1850s and sold in the form of a powder, block, or coating on a sheet of paper. The whitening agent was synthetic ultramarine, composed of clay, silica, sulfur, rosin, and charcoal.[9]

Kitchens weren't the only place where color was used in an effort to repel flies. Originally, it was common to see porch ceilings of Victorian and Colonial homes painted light blue. This was an attempt to fool flies into thinking the ceiling was actually the sky.[10]

This belief was so pervasive that it led to the development of a color from the paint manufacturer Farrow and Ball named "Cook's Blue."[11] There is still a color in their line of paints referencing this popular color. The color is a medium-value, medium-saturated blue. On their website, the company notes this color was "often found in kitchens and larders during the nineteenth century in the belief that flies never land on it."[12]

Have other places used similar saturated blues on the exterior of buildings in order to deter insects? The city of Jodhpur, in India, has many buildings that have been painted or surfaced in blue since the sixteenth century. This commonly seen color is described as "blue indigo" or "intense cobalt blue." Because its use is based on practical, religious, and cultural preferences, "the penchant here for blue has several explanations. . . [T]his color also helps to keep away mosquitoes."[13]

In other areas, this belief was so commonly accepted that one source relates: "Homespun wisdom holds, says the *Kitchen Idea Book,* that pale blue wards off flies. That's why the shade has traditionally colored porch and kitchen ceilings in the South."[14]

Despite the prevalence of this belief about the color blue, it is still difficult to pinpoint a single color that would repel all flies or, for that matter, all insects. Consider this statement about insect pollination: "Very generally, bees prefer yellows, blues, and whites; beetles prefer creams or greenish colors; flies prefer browns, purples, or greens; moths prefer reds, purples, whites, and pale pinks; butterflies prefer bright reds and purples. However, keep in mind that there are many exceptions."[15]

Controlled studies have examined the influence of color on the behavior of flies; however, the type of insect or fly and the variables being studied are not consistent. One study suggests that shape may affect the attraction of blueberry maggot flies to traps and mentions that colors may represent food or signal reproductive activity of flies.[16] Another study concludes that seasonal variation, larval host, and population origin are some factors affecting a fruit fly's attraction to particular colors.[17] Still other investigations arrive at results indicating the value dimension of a color may serve as a cue for Japanese tabanid flies.[18] This finding emphasizes the role of contrast in the visual attraction of tabanid flies, with the maximum contrast being a dark, saturated blue against grass. In a related study, researchers present a hypothesis, explaining findings in various research studies, that tsetse (Glossina) flies associate black and blue surfaces with shady resting places and settle on the black (dark) surfaces of a trap.[19] They also note that on a clear, sunny day, shadows have a blue coloration that is not noticeable to humans.[20]

In spite of this somewhat inconclusive evidence and because of the widespread practice of using blue as a fly repellant in diverse areas of the world, there remain questions that require further study. Additional controlled studies, isolating specific variables, would perhaps yield more conclusive data on the validity of the belief that blue repels flies. Nonetheless, this common practice has resulted in many blue kitchens and buildings throughout the world. It has influenced paint colors in places as diverse as St. Croix, U.S. Virgin Islands; Suffolk, England; Tuscany, Italy; Frankfurt, Germany; and Jodhpur, India. These spaces are appreciated not just for their practical color scheme but also for the resulting aesthetics of the vibrant blue color.

# Paint Pragmatics

Practical aspects of color decision making can reflect social, economic, and historical roots. At other times, color pragmatics relate to the physical properties of paints, materials, and finishes. Early in his career, Donald Kaufman, an artist living in San Francisco, began working to support himself by painting Victorian residences (1837–1901) in the Bay area. Originally painted in as many as ten contrasting hues, many of these so-called Painted Ladies, with their highly ornamental architectural styles, had fallen into a state of neglect. However, the resurgence of the New Colorist movement in San Francisco over thirty years ago returned many of the Painted Ladies to their multihued former glory.

In his experience with the Painted Ladies, Kaufman became frustrated with the quality of the paints on the market at that time and started mixing acrylics into the base latex paints he was using to produce more complex and vibrant hues. Thus began his career as an architectural colorist. Now based in New York City with collaborator Taffy Dahl, Kaufman has consulted with major museums and galleries across the country and has contributed his expertise to notable commercial and residential spaces designed by the late Philip Johnson; Charles Gwathmey; Philippe Starck; Pei, Cobb, Freed & Partners; and a host of other prominent designers and firms.[21] Not only has he created a highly respected color consultancy, but also, more recently, he has developed his own line of paint.

Kaufman finds most commercial paints less than satisfying. The standard manufacturing process uses the fewest possible pigments to create a paint color. Manufacturers work with both natural/earth and synthetic pigments. For mixing neutral paints, earth pigments include red oxide, burnt umber, yellow oxide, and lamp black. For mixing chromatic hues, synthetic pigments include Fast red, Thalo blue, and Hansa yellow. These pigments produce well-defined hues but often lack complexity. To adjust the value and intensity of the paint color, black pigment is introduced into the mixture. This approach makes paint color consistent and easy to match, and it is economical; however, commercial paint color also can lack luminosity or depth.

To create a custom wall color, Kaufman advocates intermixing pigments in small and carefully controlled amounts to create what he calls "full-spectrum" paint. The resulting hues can be tonal or saturated in hue but are complex in their composition. Never introducing black into his mixtures (black absorbs light), he advocates incorporating a small amount of a complement into the mixture when the hue needs to be toned. Full-spectrum color in interiors appears luminous, and the wall color can even appear to shift in hue depending on changes in lighting. This is caused by the complex mixtures in the paint.

Importantly, Kaufman frequently tests paint colors in the process. Paint color looks different when wet or dry. The intensity of paint color in the final installation can be hard to visualize. Lighting also has tremendous impact on color. But the effects cannot be fully predicted without knowledge of the material properties and lighting. A red paint might retain its coloration under a number of light sources, while another red may appear noticeably orange under daylighting. That is why even experienced colorists and designers often finalize paint colors at the installation sites, a process mentioned in several cases in this book.

Paint finish—matte, eggshell or satin, gloss—affects both coloration and performance. Offering the most durable finish, paints with a gloss finish also emphasize surface imperfections because of their highly reflective surface. While matte paints absorb more light, they are less durable in their finishes. A satin or eggshell finish offers a balance between matte and gloss.

Pragmatic color considerations appeared in the recent paint restoration of Fallingwater designed in 1936; over the decades, the moisture and humidity of the location—over a waterfall—led to problems with the adhesion of the paint to the building. In 2005–2006, PPG Architectural Finishes tested eight paint systems to determine which paint showed the best performance.[22] Adhesion, color, and finish were closely analyzed. Ultimately, the restoration used interior eggshell latex mixed to the exclusive Fallingwater ocher hue on both walls and ceilings in the living room, offices, and walkway. Given the high level of sunlight that consistently enters the master bedroom, a flat latex paint finish was required to lessen the sheen in this inte-

rior space. A durable gloss finish was specified for the Cherokee red metalwork. The restoration used only zero-VOC paint. Munsell color specifications gauged the exact color for concrete wall and ceiling surfaces as well as metalwork.

While the Fallingwater restoration project focused on historical accuracy and performance standards as major pragmatic drivers, the following project emphasizes another pragmatic driver: economics. For this institutional design, budget was limited, yet paint color creates a stimulating learning environment with well-differentiated interior spaces. It also illustrates principles of sustainability.

## *Educational Color: K–8 School*

This independent K–8 school is located in an economically depressed section of Newark, New Jersey (Figure 8-3a). The designers from Gensler did not set out to create a highly refined aesthetic when designing St. Philip's Academy; the economic parameters of the project did not allow for expensive finishes or precision installations. Rather, the focus remained squarely on educating children, regard-

**Figure 8-3a**
St. Philip's Academy
(Newark, New Jersey)

less of income, in an inspiring environment that optimizes teaching and learning. The school is housed in a vintage building, a former chocolate factory, and is designed sustainably. The project budget was limited, but client enthusiasm was not. With the client's full approval, the designers opted to incorporate highly saturated hues throughout the school. The only constraint was that the client did not want purple

**Figure 8-3b**
St. Philip's lobby
space illustrates
a truth-in-materials
approach

introduced as a primary color in the interior, fearing a negative psychological reaction in the students.

The school accommodates over three hundred students in a 55,000-square-foot building. The basement contains the cafeteria, a multiuse space, and administrative offices (Figures 8-3b, c). Kindergarten and first grade are housed on the first floor; second through fourth grades are located on the second floor; fifth and sixth grades are situated on the third floor; and seventh and eighth grades are on the top floor of the building.

The metaphor for the interior coloration aligns with the curriculum: Earth as school. Intense warm colors represent the inner earth (lower grades), while the visual temperature becomes cooler and less saturated when reaching toward the stratosphere (the upper grades). The primary coloration from floor to floor shifts from red and yellow-orange to yellow and from yellow-green to blue (Figures 8-3d–f). Each floor has two main colors within the classroom, with a third color in the corridors and transitional spaces. Each palette is unique to the floor and is equal in saturation. The team drew color inspiration from an out-of-print book that illustrates patterns in nature and expanded the concept of a living Earth. According to Dana Jenkins, design principal, "We took a different approach to how we applied these colors. The primary color fills the space and the window walls. We incorporated a contrasting color below the sill line. The colors next to one another create unusual combinations and create an invigorating harmony rather than a cacophony."

Each floor contains four to six classrooms with windows, as incorporating natural light into these spaces became a priority in the renovation; the designers based their decision on research indicating that natural light correlates with better information retention. The project includes a new environmental center on top of the gymnasium that is designed as an education and activity center. Part of the environmental center includes a vegetable and herb garden, where students plant food to be harvested for

*Opposite*
**Figure 8-3c**
St. Philip's cafeteria
contains renovated
and existing materials
and finishes

Color Planning for Interiors

use in the cafeteria (Figures 8-3g, h). Within the cafeteria, students eat meals family-style, and organic waste is pulped and composted for use in the roof garden. The entire growing cycle is contained on the premises as a closed loop. This offers important opportunities for learning, particularly in the urban setting.

Because of the limited budget and in keeping with sustainable design practices, materials selection and restoration options were minimized. While it was cost-prohibitive to restore the damaged original wood flooring, the designers were able to embrace the existing heavy timber structure and brick to unify the interior and the architecture. The materials palette included paint, ceramic tile, and resilient flooring.

A graphics program is planned for later completion; ideally, each floor will have a large graphic in the hallways. A gigantic head of a chameleon, for example, would be installed on one large wall. Up close, the wall will appear swathed in an abstract pattern of highly pixilated colors, but the eye of the chameleon will come into sharp focus as one steps back from the mural, illustrating the process of optical mixing.

*Opposite*

*Top* **Figure 8-3d**
St. Philip's lower school has a classroom with a tint of red-orange wall color

*Bottom* **Figure 8-3e**
St. Philip's lower school contains a saturated yellow classroom with bright artwork

**Figure 8-3f**
St. Philip's upper school has a blue science lab

Working within myriad pragmatic constraints, Gensler created an energetic, exciting environment in which to learn and teach. This building affects the educational experience for children, teachers, and administrators and has brought about change in the Newark community. Since St. Philip's was completed, new homes have sprung up in its vicinity, helping revitalize this area of the city.

St. Philip's is the first LEED-certified academic building in Newark, and it garnered a New Jersey Smart Growth award for positive neighborhood impact. The school has begun to integrate sustainable strategies into everyday experiences. Teachers are developing curricula about the facility and the neighborhood. Some students' families are taking another look at how they eat. Administrators are working to align themselves with likeminded foundations and vendors. It is exciting to see how the process brought systemic change to this institution, elevating it to a new standard.

St. Philip's shows how much can be accomplished within a constrained budget. Color, lighting, and materiality also contributed to the charge of creating a sustainable building. The designers addressed pragmatic issues of sustainability through the

**Figure 8-3h**
St. Philip's site offers a natural learning environment

*Opposite*
**Figure 8-3g**
St. Philip's green transition space visually relates to the garden space

*Color for Pragmatics*          181

introduction of daylight into the classrooms, the reuse of existing materials in the renovated space, and the development of a green roof.

# Sustainable Strategies

St. Phillip's Academy illustrates ways that designers consider color pragmatically to address sustainability in a project with budget constraints. Similarly, sustainability surfaced as a major driver in the showrooms by HOK and in the Affinity pediatric clinic designed by FLAD Architects. Ultimately, the school, showrooms, and clinic were LEED-certified and offer lessons on sustainability. Nearly all specified materials contained at least 25 percent recycled content and at St. Phillip's, existing brick and wood gleaned from the renovation were reused in other parts of the new addition. Further, in the Allsteel/Gunlocke resource centers, all materials were either locally derived or extracted no more than 500 miles from the project site. Not only is this a sustainable strategy, but the use of such materials also reinforces regionalism and a sense of place. Across the projects, U.S. Green Building Council emission standards guided paint specification. The designers employed a similar process of having the first coat of paint applied onsite to evaluate and adjust the color temperature and value under different lighting conditions. Shifts in natural light can produce greater variation in wall color than more controlled illumination, making on-site color testing critical in sustainable projects.

A hallmark of sustainable design is an abundance of natural lighting for conserving energy. In the sustainable projects contained in this book, lighting and color worked together with the aim of enhancing learning in a K-8 school, showcasing new project lines in three resource centers, and facilitating the comfort and diagnosis of patients in a pediatric clinic. In contrast with the school and clinic, the designers of the Allsteel/Gunlocke resource centers had the additional challenge of an open space plan. The goal was to effectively illuminate featured furniture products using an energy-efficient system. Large fenestration filtered natural light into the open interior which offered a primary source of illumination during the daytime. A dimming system with photo sensors was specified for all lighting, using fixtures with metal halide lamps and ballasts, for better lighting at reduced wattages that could be used during the day and at night for evening events. This carefully considered lighting plan resulted in 50 percent less lighting power density than is the industry standard.

Finding innovative ways to design sustainably with color and lighting remains a challenge. For progressive designers, firms, and clients, the commitment to sustainable design continues to grow unabated, but does require the design practitioner to commit to new ideas, experimentation, and testing as well as keeping current on industry developments in color finishes, materials, and lighting. Perhaps the next generation of designers will not focus primarily on sustainability on a project-by-project basis, but will rethink the meaning of socially responsible design and its implications for consumption patterns and expectations.

Certain practice areas, such as showroom design, expect that the interior setting is reworked annually, with major renovations occurring in a three- to five-year cycle. In other sectors, including institutional design, expectations for renovation, particularly in schools, often extend for decades. Perhaps industry norms for interior renovations should be reconsidered along with color trends and cycles to optimize the conservation of environmental resources.

# Summary

This chapter describes pragmatic considerations in color planning. Economics, material quality, and design preconditions all enter the color planning process and deserve explicit recognition. As technology evolves, new materials and surface finishes will become ever more ambitious, as will the means of measuring and standardizing these finishes. The momentum of sustainable design clearly affects pragmatic color use today. Sustainable materials and light solutions are integrally tied to color. The project narrative in this chapter describes the color planning process for a school design that emphasizes pragmatics in addition to compositional, communicative, and engagement criteria.

**NOTES**

1. Susanka, *Creating the Not-So-Big House*, 248–249.
2. Swirnoff, *The Color of Cities*.
3. Lenclos and Lenclos, *Colors of the World*.
4. Personal communication, August 2006.
5. cc.msnscache.com/cache

*continues*

6.  www.tuscanestates.com/tuscany_la_foce_gonzola.php

7.  Abbe, "Kitchen Artistry."

8.  www.victorian-society.org.uk/adv12.html

9.  www.frankjump.com/002.html

10. www.art-first.com/12inthemedia.html

11. www.thisoldhouse.com/toh/knowhow/interiors/article/0,16417,1125378,00.html

12. www.farrow-ball.com/productdetails.aspx?pid=0237CB&cid=PC&language=en-GB

13. Lenclos and Lenclos.

14. www.kitchens.com/Remodeling-And-Design/Products-and-materials/walls-mouldings/default.asp

15. cnps-yerbabuena.org/gard_saul_ger_pollination.html

16. Liburd, Alm, Casagrande, and Polavarapu, "Effect of Trap Color, Bait, Shape, and Orientation in Attraction of Blueberry Maggot (diptera: tephritidae) Flies."

17. Ibid.

18. Sasaki, "Comparison of Capturing Tabanid Flies (diptera: tabanidae) by Five Different Color Traps in the Fields."

19. Steverding and Troscianko, "On the Role of Blue Shadows in the Visual Behaviour of Tsetse Flies," S17.

20. Ibid., S16.

21. Kaufman and Dahl, *Color: Natural Palettes for Painted Rooms.*

22. Jerome, Weiss, and Ephon, "Fallingwater Part 2."

# Color Criteria in Concert

*We know, in fact, that colour can be made to work for its living—to make
objects look heavier (or lighter), space to seem warmer (or cooler), planes to
advance or recede. . . . It can be used to signal or delineate, to stimulate or
depress, to give a sense of place and thus a sense of identity.*

—Sir Hugh Casson

## Color Processes Revealed

In the final analysis, the way in which the designer approaches color is vital. "Designers who consider place as an experience, or as part of a social domain, will address the
design task differently than those who treat it as an object to be colored."[1] A recent
study of recognized Australian designers described their use of color as "context-
sensitive," "innovative," "thoughtful," and "end-user-sensitive."[2] "Context-sensitive"
suggests an integration of color, space, and form. It also implies responsiveness to
the architecture and site conditions. "Innovative" suggests imaginative, original, and

appropriate color use. "Thoughtful" implies a reflective and careful consideration of color in the process, while "end-user-sensitive" recognizes the human responses to color.

The noted designers in the study also reported what they perceived as the functions of architectural color. They saw color as most strongly contributing to building form and perceptions of space, followed by ambiance and orientation. These findings support color composition, communication, and engagement in the color planning framework. However, the framework defines behavioral aspects of color more broadly than wayfinding or spatial orientation, and it recognizes color pragmatics and preferences as well.

The Australian designers recognized that color in certain project types, such as healthcare design, may have more impact than in others. While this may be difficult to quantify, color decisions for a neonatal intensive care unit, for example, must be approached more cautiously than in many other design contexts.

Regardless of project type, noted environmental color consultant Werner Spillman advocates considering color early in the design process and throughout three phases of development. He maintains the initial phase of conceptualizing color should focus on psychological and physical issues, followed by detailed planning, which leads to multiple color proposals and ends in realization of materials composing the color palette. His process focuses on human needs, project specifics, and materiality but does not specifically address lighting, pragmatic, or preference issues.

The last narrative in this book illustrates the color planning criteria holistically in the design process and concludes with a narrative that captures a firsthand experience in a dynamic color- and light-filled space. Learning from such cases helps bring principles of color to life.

# Experiential Color: Designing the Aquarium

This case recounts the process of designing a precedent-setting space for experiencing marine life. The intent was to create an aquarium of world-class excellence. Innovations in color, lighting, and materiality were central in supporting a new vision of the Georgia Aquarium, which draws record-breaking crowds. The existing precedent for the design of aquariums typically left much to be desired. The interior design of such environments in previous generations entailed nondescript concrete and glass enclosures where visitors often moved through exhibitions in a unidirectional line under less than optimal lighting conditions. A completely different type of aquarium was wanted in Atlanta.

Design a world-class aquarium—the charge to the tvsdesign designers could not be more straightforward. The client, Bernard Marcus, wanted to build the biggest and best aquarium in the world. Yet the heroic scale of the space was not the only challenge; the aquarium was to offer a singularly memorable experience to all who visited it. Marcus once again posed a plain directive to the designers: "I want every person who enters the aquarium to have a wow experience!" The client, who cofounded Home Depot in 1978, had a reputation as a visionary thinker and one who liked to get things done. Marcus was intently focused on giving back to the city of Atlanta, which had served as the home base to his company headquarters for nearly three decades. His appreciation of innovation and sense of urgency were palpable; he would settle for no less than setting a new design standard.

In the early phases of design development, a personal friend of the client saw the shape of an ark in some of the preliminary conceptual sketches. The idea of an ark resonated with Marcus, who seized upon the idea, but the design team was less than enthusiastic about the potentially limiting qualities of a representational image. Ultimately, an abstraction of the ark offered an ideal gateway for the massing and spatial configuration of the building. Figure 9-1 illustrates an exterior iteration of the abstracted ark.

**Figure 9-1**
Georgia Aquarium, exterior view (Atlanta)

The interior architecture offered visitors an immersion, theater-like experience, recalls Steve Clem, tvsdesign principal. The design team agreed the concept of a sea mount could guide the organization of interior spaces. Sea mounts are sheltered underwater enclaves whose warm currents draw large aggregates of varied sea life. These environmental havens elicit a sense of wonder and represent an underwater equivalent of the Galapagos Islands. This concept translates spatially into a core with radiating spaces

*Right* **Figure 9-2a**
LED fully programmable
light sequence offers
low-level lighting
and fluidity relating
to water in an aquatic
environment

*Bottom Left* **Figure 9-2b**
Lighting detail (blue)

*Bottom Right* **Figure 9-2c**
Lighting detail (green)

Color Planning for Interiors

*Top Left* **Figure 9-2d**
Lighting detail
(blue-green)

*Top Right* **Figure 9-2e**
Lighting detail
(orange to green

*Left* **Figure 9-2f**
Lighting detail (white)

*Color Criteria in Concert*

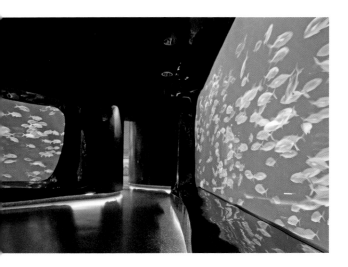

centering on themes of marine life—Cold Water Quest, Georgia Explorer, Ocean Voyager, River Scout, and Tropical Diver.

The six gallery spaces wrap around a central area designed as a visitor oasis. This space, called the Rotunda, allows natural light to filter into the interior through a large circular skylight. Between visits to the adjacent marine galleries, visitors can come up for air, so to speak, in the Rotunda. Although a portion of this space is well lit, other parts are quite dark. Some ambient light is provided by a large curvilinear lighting fixture that wraps around the ceiling and kinetically shifts from hue to hue, echoing the underwater motion of color and light. Figures 9-2a–f capture the kinetic shift of colored light illuminating the Rotunda.

The materiality in this central space includes terrazzo blue flooring with flecks of mother-of-pearl that offer a sparkling luminescence. A wall mosaic of blue and white tiles suggests air bubbles breaking to the water's surface. Expressive color fills the Rotunda; shades of blue obviously reference water; saturated oranges relate to aquatic life. (The designers reject the notion that the orange references the Home Depot logo.)

The light-filled Rotunda feels alive with the complementary oranges and blues in a sea of textures and materials. The dim lighting in the tonal blue gallery spaces creates an under-the-sea experience for the visitors and showcases many exhibits. The lighting levels support the health and well-being of the marine life housed in the gallery tanks. The overall contrast of light and dark defines activity zones within the interior. In the low-lit gallery spaces, the lighting supports the viewing experience, while higher lighting levels allow for talking, resting, eating, and shopping in the Rotunda. A variety of lighting conditions illuminates the interiors appearing in Figures 9-3–5.

The natural light and brighter coloration in the central space offer psychological relief from the intense viewing experiences in the aquatic galleries. Again, the intent is for visitors to view exhibitions and then regroup in the Rotunda before returning to the marine galleries. A large circular skylight illuminates a café adjacent to the exhibition spaces (see Figures 9-6–8). Figure 9-9 shows the attention to detail in the specification and design of interior materials and finishes.

The retail stores extend the aquarium experience. Exhibition and museum spaces often position their retail stores near the exit of the building. This project contains two retail spaces: a large shop close to the exit and a small one in the Rotunda. The smaller shop was conceived of as a gallery space on par with the marine galleries, creating a continuous experience.

The color vocabulary in the retail spaces consists of dark blues representing water, greens symbolizing sea kelp, and oranges signifying vibrant sea life. Column elements within the shops contain backlit translucent fabrics that conceal fully programmable colored LCD lighting. Similar to the lighting elements in the Rotunda, this decorative lighting shifts in coloration. Likewise, a serpentine wall within the retail interior creates a sense of energy and life. The location of the smaller retail shop in the Rotunda facilitates quick transactions for buying souvenirs, disposable cameras, and bottled drinks. The shop is more child oriented than the larger retail venue near the exit. Merchandise is organized by color blocking.

**Figure 9-6**
Light-dark boundaries are clearly demarcated between the Rotunda and marine gallery spaces

*Opposite*
**Figure 9-7**
Skylight brings natural lighting into the Rotunda

**Figure 9-8**
Variations of orange
and blue coexist in
white surrounds

The second floor contains limited-access space that serves the teaching and outreach mission of the aquarium. The spatial organization facilitates the flow of visitors and the quality of their experience. Large school groups rotate between floors to visit hands-on learning rooms and to view exhibits shown in Figure 9-10, 9-11.

Other limited-access spaces on the second floor accommodate research scientists. Additionally, Figure 9-12 illustrates a large ballroom hosting private group events held after normal hours of operation. This level of the aquarium gives the aquarium true flexibility of function.

What were the main lessons learned from the project? Significantly, color, lighting, and materiality all contribute to the emotional draw of the space. Early in the design process, the TVS designers invested in an extensive process of "image benchmarking," where they studied a range of interiors characterized by a strong ambiance rather than focusing on aquarium design per se. They also held in-house charettes and design reviews to explore and critique ideas. The designers worked within a generous budget but had to complete the project on an aggressive time schedule of thirty months.

*Opposite*
**Figure 9-9**
Color and materiality
in wall and upholstered
seating detail reference
water movement
and sea life

196        Color Planning for Interiors

The monumental scale of the space initially posed a challenge to the design team, prompting them to consider, "How do you create large spaces yet retain a sense of intimacy?" Color offered a way to sculpt the grand Rotunda to create a more human scale before entering the more compressed gallery spaces. Further, the team had the opportunity and resources to explore materials that significantly enhanced the design. Clem notes how the materials palette includes colored glass and terrazzo with embedded mother-of-pearl, not only creating textural interest but also meeting high performance standards. He further describes the "waterside" flooring, a dark blue terrazzo, as suggesting water ripples and reflections. The "beachside" flooring, a sand-colored quartz tile, implies a shoreline and offers traction on a floor ramp for visitors who use wheelchairs. These reflective and matte materials and surface finishes enrich the palette and heighten the sense of detail.

# Color Interpretation

Multiple color criteria surface in the design of the Georgia Aquarium: color as human response, color as composition, color as communication, and color as pragmatics:

- *Human response*—Creating a memorable and engaging experience where visitors increase their understanding of marine life, flow easily through zones of activity, and want to return to the setting.
- *Compositional form*—Creating focal points and areas of emphasis as well as a sense of progression through the color and materials palette. Color and lighting create a feeling of human scale within a monumental space.

- *Associative meaning*—Communicating the ambiance of an underwater environment reflects the sea mount concept. This experience is tempered with areas for restoration.
- *Pragmatic considerations*—Specifying high-performance materials for durability and maintenance. Addressing visibility needs of the visitors and meeting the low lighting requirement for the sea life.

The Georgia Aquarium offers a setting in which to experience a range of species in relatively close physical contact. Color in the interior architecture influences visitors psychologically and behaviorally. The contrast between light and dark immediately defines spaces for engagement, learning, and respite. The dimly lit, monotone galleries house exhibits and offer ideal settings for viewing. Of paramount importance, their lighting and coloration support the well-being of the marine life on view.

Daylighting from a skylight fills the Rotunda and creates a natural gathering space for visitors for respite and regrouping. This central space is filled with light and defined by color, pattern, and texture. Settings that do not place high demand on thinking and concentration can have more contrasting colors and a stimulating design, referred to as a *high-load environment.* Conversely, the minimalistic marine galleries allow the visitors to focus and process information; this type of setting is called a *low-load environment.*

Throughout the aquarium, color supports experiential learning and orients visitors from exhibition to exhibition. Color in the interior also conjures associations of an underwater world using the specific concept of a sea mount. Color associations relate blues to water, greens to sea kelp, and contrasting oranges and red-violets to exotic fish and sea corals. Color and light offer a significant way to create the sense of wonder expected by the client. The design did, in fact, exceed his expectations.

Another role of color in the aquarium is compositional. Color interacts with the interior architecture to shape the monumental space by conveying the human scale within it. In addition to light-dark contrasts, the aquarium contains numerous examples of cold-warm contrast. These visual temperature contrasts surface within a single hue and between analogous colors such as orange, red-orange, and yellow-orange. Still other temperature contrasts are found between the complementary colors blue and orange. The range of temperature modulations shows a nuanced understanding of color.

Color progressions also emerge in the additive mixing of lights that change from one hue to the next throughout the spectrum. Colored lighting glows from a stretched fabric surface ensconcing ceiling and column elements. These lit elements progress from blue to green to orange and magenta in the Rotunda and the retail spaces, drawing attention to the ceiling and column elements. Color affects visitors directly, communicates the feeling of an aquatic environment, and addresses pragmatic realities. By integrating color, lighting, and materiality into a well-conceived architectural form, the Georgia Aquarium captures the sense of a dynamic aquatic environment.

# Experiencing Interior Color: Inside-Out

*I'd like to be under the sea in an octopus's garden in the shade.*

—The Beatles

The following narrative, written by Julia Sexton for this book, reflects the subjective experience of color. During her junior year as an interior design student, Julia traveled with her class to hear about the process of creating the Georgia Aquarium directly from the designers at TVS who created the space before experiencing the aquarium itself.

## *The Georgia Aquarium Experience*
My expectations couldn't have been higher after leaving the firm, where I heard about the behind-the-scenes process of designing the Georgia Aquarium from TVS principal Donna Childs and her collaborators. After presenting the project, Childs and her colleagues explained the more technical aspects of the project and responded to our questions regarding technical details such as the number of gallons in the largest tank and the thickness of the glass in the tanks. Learning about the technology that went into the construction of the facility fascinated me.

What caught me by surprise, when entering the Aquarium, was the lighting. Each space in the aquarium seems to require a different approach to lighting. In the large tank-viewing area, the light comes from the tank itself. Natural light filters through the water, creating a lovely blue glow with the movement of the water against the walls and surrounding areas. In the core rotunda space, a large skylight fills the open space with natural lighting. This, along with the overall lighting and coloration of the room, creates a bluish ambiance, which in effect echoes the feeling of being underwater.

Each of the five gallery spaces—Cold Water Quest, Georgia Explorer, Ocean Voyager, River Scout, and Tropical Diver—has individual characteristics that display wildlife in a small-scale setting of natural habitat. The unique nature of each individual space calls for equally unique lighting conditions. I think the goal of most exhibition-type space is to showcase the artwork—or, in this case, the animals and their habitats. TVS created spaces with low lighting so the animals and their homes are displayed with a level of intensity that left me truly amazed. I remember being mesmerized by a smaller exhibit of bright reddish-orange jellyfish backlit by a blue screen. There I stood, transfixed, for at least twenty minutes, watching the jellyfish lazily float about in this exhibit built like a window into the walkway. It is a small part of the aquarium, but I felt like I was spying through a window into an alien world, seeing these translucent creatures in a new backdrop.

Designing an aquarium clearly offers creative license for color, and TVS exploited every available opportunity for innovative applications. For me, the most memorable use of color was the large band of light glowing from the upper portions of nearly every wall in the rotunda. These bands changed color from blue to green to yellow to red to purple in a rolling effect, like a wave crashing. In an unexpected way, the lighting and color created a kind of rhythm throughout the space, and I remember feeling the sensation of being underwater due to the combination of the timing of the color changes and the flow of lighting. Thinking back to the aquarium, I immediately get a sense of being cooled off.

The natural habitats of the animals allowed for a more experimental color palette than would be found in many other types of interiors. And because this is such a special environment, the typical boundaries usually set up for color were practically nonexistent. I noticed how well the designers of the aquarium balanced the color between the exhibits and the transitional spaces. It would have been easy to overdo it with color, but by keeping a relatively high-key palette in which white is punctuated with splashes of color, areas outside the marine galleries seem to offer just the right amount of stimulation.

It was evident to me that the design team implemented at least three of the five color planning criteria when designing the aquarium. The ones I saw most clearly utilized were color as a formal design element that helps shape the space, color as communication that aids in developing the concept, and color that influences human behavior and responses. The three criteria can be witnessed throughout the space. To me, the second criterion is the most successful. The main goal of the firm was to create a space that would wow its audience and make visitors feel as though they were underwater. Thus, implementing color as a communication tool that aids in developing the concept was the most effective way to accomplish that goal.

Another aspect that struck me was the scale and relationship of spaces. The large rotunda forms the core and the main circulation space between the exhibits. The exhibit spaces radiate off the core and create a sense of scale and proportion. I thought that, in a way, the layout relates to the variety of animals and sea life at the aquarium, from the largest fish in the world, the whale shark, to the smallest piece of coral. I also remember being impressed by the sense of scale differentiating the two retail spaces.

Of course there is always a bottom line to consider, and the Georgia Aquarium is not an exception. As at most zoos, aquariums, theme parks, and museums, the only way to exit is through the gift shop. In this aquarium, the space contains a large gift shop near the exit and a smaller one in the Rotunda. The larger gift shop, called Beyond the Reef, has a distinctive color palette of chartreuse yellow-green in the ceiling and blue all around. The exposed ceiling above the green suspended ceiling is a dark blue that resembles the deep ocean, and the design of the shape mimics the terrazzo flooring, using shades of the same colors.

Though the larger shop has all the bells and whistles, it was the smaller shop, called Sand Dollars, that got my attention. This smaller retail space was designed in a way that was subtle but beautiful. The flooring consists of different colors of terrazzo laid out in fluid and organic configurations. The walls are clad with white mosaic tiles, plus blue, green, and orange tiles that are densely present at the base and fan out as they go up the wall, like air bubbles moving toward the surface of water. This space, with its restrained detailing, has a boutique feel due to its size.

What do I remember most vividly from my time at the Georgia Aquarium?

As a student of interior design, I noticed how well the lighting and color created an ambiance for supporting the extensive collection of marine life and their habitats. I remember how this space celebrates the wonders of the oceans, rivers, and streams of this beautiful planet. It is a haven of natural beauty in an unnatural setting that complements the ecosystems around us and teaches us about the animals we know and love. Who wouldn't want that?

*. . . And who can't wait to see how the power of color is expressed by Julia and reinterpreted by a new emerging cohort of designers?*

## NOTES

1. Smith, "Environmental Colouration and/or the Design Process," 360.
2. Ibid.

# Bibliography

Abbe, Mary. "Kitchen Artistry." *Star Tribune,* Section F, July 30, 2006: 3.

Albers, Josef. *Interaction of Color,* rev. ed. New Haven, CT: Yale University Press, 2006.

Aslam, Mubeen. "Are You Selling the Right Colour? A Cross-cultural Review of Colour as a Marketing Cue." *Journal of Marketing Communications* 12, no. 1 (2006): 15–30.

Beach, L. R., B. K. Wise, and J. A. Wise. *The Human Factors of Color in Environmental Decisions: A Critical Review.* National Aeronautics and Space Administration document, 1998.

Benke, Britta. *O'Keeffe.* London: Benedikt Taschen Verlag, 2000.

Berlin, Brent, and Paul Kay. *Basic Color Terms: Their Universality and Evolution.* Berkeley: University of California Press, 1969.

Beyer, Oskar(ed) *Eric Mendelsohn: Letters of an Architect.* New York: Abelard-Schuman, 1967.

Birren, Faber. *Color and Human Response.* New York: John Wiley and Sons, 1984.

Boeschenstein, William. "Expressive Urban Color." *Journal of Architectural Planning Research* 3. (1976): 275–285.

Busse, Laura Compton. *Responses to Color in Workplace Environments: Narratives of Designers, Managers, and Employees.* Unpublished master's thesis. Lexington: University of Kentucky, 2002.

Carpman, Janet, and Myron Grant. *Design That Cares: Planning Health Facilities for Patients and Visitors,* rev. ed. New York: John Wiley and Sons, 1991.

Dohr, Joy, and Margaret Portillo. "Color in Design Education: New Approaches Beyond the Bauhaus." In *Aspects of Color,* edited by E. Hamalainen and H. Arnkil, 67–74. Helsinki, Finland: UIAH University Printing House, 1995.

Dunn, Maria Soledad. *Color Criteria in Cross-cultural Symbolism: Case Research of Noted Designers in Ecuador.* Unpublished master's thesis. Lexington: University of Kentucky,1996.

Elliot, Andrew, Markus Maier, Arlene Moller, Ron Friedman, and Jorg Meinhardt. "Color and Psychological Functioning: The Effect of Red on Performance Attainment." *Journal of Experimental Psychology: General* 136, no. 1 (2007): 154–168.

Eysenck, Hans. "A Critical and Experimental Study of Color Preferences." *American Journal of Psychology* (1941): 49–57.

Fallingwater Archives. Fallingwater, Western Pennsylvania Conservancy, Mill Run, PA.

Finlay, Victoria. *Color: A Natural History of the Palette.* New York: Random House, 2002.

Harkness, Nick. "The Colour Wheels of Art, Perception, Science, and Physiology." *Optics and Laser Technology* 38, no. 4–6 (2006): 219–229.

Heifetz, Jeanne. *When Blue Meant Yellow: How Colors Got Their Names.* New York: Henry Holt, 1994.

Hoegg, JoAndrea, and Joseph W. Alba. "Taste Perception: More Than Meets the Tongue." *Journal of Consumer Research,* 71 (2007): 12–25.

Hoffmann, Donald. *Frank Lloyd Wright's Fallingwater: The House and Its History.* New York: Dover, 1978.

Hope, Augustine, and Margaret Walch, eds. *The Color Compendium.* New York: Van Nostrand Reinhold, 1990.

Hornung, David. *Color: A Workshop Approach.* New York: McGraw-Hill, 2005.

Hovers, Erella, Shimon Ilani, Ofer Bar-Yosef, and Bernard Vandermeersch. "An Early Case of Color Symbolism: Ochre Use by Modern Humans in Qafzeh Cave." *Current Anthropology* 44, no. 4 (2003): 491–522.

Hunt, David. "Colour Symbolism in the Folk Literature of the Caucasus." *Folklore* 117 (2006): 329–338.

Hutchings, John. "Colour in Folklore and Tradition: The Principles." *Color Research and Application* 29, no. 1 (2004): 57–66.

Isahara, Shinobu. *The Series of Plates Designed as a Test for Colour Deficiency.* Tokyo: Kanehara Trading, 2004.

Itten, Johannes. *The Art of Color: The Subjective Experience and Objective Rationale of Color.* New York: John Wiley and Sons, 1986.

———. *The Color Star.* New York: John Wiley and Sons, 1986.

Jerome, Pamela, Norman Weiss, and Hazel Ephon. "Fallingwater Part 2: Materials—Conservation at Frank Lloyd Wright's Masterpiece." *APT Bulletin: Journal of Preservation Technology* 37, 2–3 (2006): 9.

Kahn, Barbara E., and Brian Wansink. "The Influence of Assortment Structure on Perceived Variety and Consumption Quantities." *Journal of Consumer Research* 30, (2004): 519–533.

Kaufman, Donald, and Taffy Dahl, text by Laurel Graeber. *Color: Natural Palettes for Painted Rooms.* New York: Crown, 1992.

Kaufmann, Edgar, Jr. *Fallingwater: A Frank Lloyd Wright Country House.* New York: Abbeville, 1986.

Kay, Paul, and Brent Berlin. "There Are Non-trivial Constraints on Color Categorization." *Brain and Behavioral Sciences* 20 (1997): 196–202.

Kaya, Naz, and Melanie Crosby. "Color Associations with Different Building Types: An Experimental Study in American College Students." *Color Research and Application* 31, no. 1 (2006): 67–71.

Kaya, Naz, and Helen Epps. "Relationship Between Color and Emotion: A Study of College Students." *College Student Journal* 38 (2004): 396–405.

Kelly, Rob Roy. "Recollections of Josef Albers." *Design Issues* 16, no. 2 (2000): 3–24.

Knoblauch, Kenneth. "On Quantifying the Bipolarity and Axis of the Farnsworth-Munsell 100-Hue Test." *Investigative Ophthalmology and Visual Science* 28 (1987): 707–710.

Kushwah, Tripti. *Lighting in the Design Process: Toward a Framework of Interpretive Lighting.* Unpublished master's thesis. Lexington: University of Kentucky, 2004.

Kwallek, Nancy, Kokyung Soon, and Carol Lewis. "Workweek Productivity, Visual Complexity, and Individual Environmental Sensitivity in Three Offices of Different Color Interiors." *Color Research and Application* 32, no. 2 (2007): 130–143.

Lenclos, Jean-Philippe, and Dominique Lenclos. *Colors of the World: The Geography of Color.* New York: W. W. Norton, 2004.

Liburd, O. E., S. R. Alm, R. A. Casagrande, and S. Polavarapu. "Effect of Trap Color, Bait, Shape, and Orientation in Attraction of Blueberry Maggot (diptera: tephritidae) Flies." *Journal of Economic Entomology* 91, no. 1 (1998): 248.

Linton, Harold, and Ron Rochon. *Color Model Environments: Color and Light in Three-dimensional Design.* New York: Van Nostrand Reinhold, 1985.

Mahnke, Frank, and Rudolf Mahnke. *Color and Light in Man-made Environments.* New York: Van Nostrand Reinhold, 1987.

Meerwin, Gerhard, Bettina Rodeck, and Frank Mahnke. *Color: Communication in Architectural Space.* Berlin: Birkhauser, 2007.

*Munsell Book of Color 2.5R-10RP: Matte Collection.* New Windsor, NY: Gretag Macbeth, 2005.

Newark, Tim. *Camouflage.* New York: Granada Paladin, 2007.

Pantone Matching System, © **COLOR**INSPIRATION/2007, swatch book.

Papenek, Victor. *Design for the Real World: Human Ecology and Social Change.* New York: Granada Paladin, 1974.

Park, Youngsoon, and Denise Guerin. "Meaning and Preference of Interior Color Palettes among Four Cultural Groups." *Journal of Interior Design* 28 (2002): 27–39.

Pasanella, Marco. "Room to Improve: The Uncolor Solution." *New York Times,* Section F, May 1, 2003: 1.

Porter, Tom, and Bryan Milellides. *Color for Architecture.* New York: Van Nostrand Reinhold, 1976.

Portillo, Margaret. *Integrating Color and Creative Vision: Color Criteria in the Design Process.* Unpublished doctoral dissertation. Madison: University of Wisconsin, 1991.

———. "A Study of Color Criteria Used by Noted Designers." *Journal of Interior Design Education and Research* 18, no. 1–2 (1992): 17–24.

Portillo, Margaret, and Joy Dohr. "Bridging Process and Structure Through Color Criteria." *Design Studies* 15, no. 4 (1994): 403–416.

Raney, Patricia. *Color Development: Dimensional Variation and Creative Elaboration.* Unpublished master's thesis. Madison: University of Wisconsin, 1992.

Rapoport, Amos, and A. Rapoport. "Color Preferences, Color Harmony, and Quantitative Use of Color." *Empirical Studies for the Arts* 2 (1984): 95–118.

Rosefelt, M. M. O. *The Design Dilemma: A Study of the New Morality of Industrial Design in Western Societies.* Unpublished doctoral dissertation. New York University, 1986.

Sasaki, Hitoshi. "Comparison of Capturing Tabanid Flies (diptera: tabanidae) by Five Different Color Traps in the Fields." *Applied Entomology and Zoology* 36, no. 4 (2001): 518.

Sattler, Madeline. *A Method for Analyzing Three-dimensional Color Interaction.* Unpublished master's thesis. Madison: University of Wisconsin, 1992.

Saunders, Barbara, and J. van Brakel. "Are There Non-trivial Constraints on Colour Categorization?" *Behavioral and Brain Sciences* 20, no. 167 (1997): 228.

Smith, Dianne. "Environmental Colouration and/or the Design Process." *Color Research and Application* 28, no. 5 (2003): 360–365.

Spillman, Werner. "Color Order Systems and Architectural Color Design." *Color Research and Application* 10, no. 1 (1985): 5–11.

Steverding, Dietmar, and Tom Troscianko. "On the Role of Blue Shadows in the Visual Behaviour of Tsetse Flies." *Proceedings: Biological Sciences* 271, Biology Letters Supplement 3 (2004): 27.

Susanka, Sarah. *Creating the Not-So-Big House: Insights and Ideas for the New American Home.* New Town, CT: Taunton, 2001.

Swirnoff, Lois. "Experiments on the Interaction of Color and Form." *Leonardo* 9 (1974): 191–195.

———. *The Color of Cities: An International Perspective.* New York: McGraw-Hill, 2000.

———. *Dimensional Color,* 2nd ed. New York: W. W. Norton, 2003.

Tate, Allen, and C. Ray Smith. *Interior Design in the 20th Century.* New York: Harper & Row, 1986.

Turner, Joy Luke. *The Munsell Color System: A Language for Color.* New York: Fairchild Press, 1996.

Verriest, Guy, J. Van Laethem, and A. Uvijls. "A New Assessment of the Normal Ranges of the Farnsworth-Munsell 100-Hue Test Scores." *American Journal of Ophthalmology* 93 (1982): 835–842.

Wheeler, Alina. *Designing Brand Identity.* Hoboken, NJ: John Wiley and Sons, 2003.

Wichmann, Felix, Lindsay Sharpe, and Karl Gegenfurtner. "The Contributions of Color to Recognition Memory for Natural Sciences." *Journal of Experimental Psychology: Learning, Memory, and Cognition* 28 (2002): 509–520.

Wright, Frank Lloyd. "In the Cause of Architecture III: The Meaning of Materials—Stone." *Architectural Record* 63 (May 1928): 350.

———. "In the Cause of Architecture IV: The Meaning of Materials—Wood." *Architectural Record* 63 (May 1928): 481, 485.

———. "Frank Lloyd Wright." *Architectural Forum* 68 (January 1938): 102.

———. *The Natural House.* New York: Horizon, 1954.

Zakia, Richard. *Perception and Imaging,* 2nd ed. Woburn, MA: Butterworth-Heinemann, 2002.

cc.msnscache.com/cache

www.tuscanestates.com/tuscany_la_foce_gonzola.php

www.victorian-society.org.uk/adv12.html

www.frankjump.com/002.html

www.art-first.com/12inthemedia.html

www.thisoldhouse.com/toh/knowhow/interiors/article/0,16417,1125378,00.html

www.farrow-ball.com/productdetails.aspx?pid=0237CB&cid=PC&language=en-GB

www.kitchens.com/Remodeling-And-Design/Products-and-materials/walls-mouldings/default.asp

cnps-yerbabuena.org/gard_saul_ger_pollination.html

# Design and Photography Credits

## CHAPTER 3

3-1  Siriporn Kobnithikulwong
3-2  Photo by Brian Gassel/TVS
3-3  Siriporn Kobnithikulwong
3-4  Amy Chen
3-5  Photo by Brian Gassel/TVS
3-6  Photo by Brian Gassel/TVS
3-7  Photo by Brian Gassel/TVS
3-8  Siriporn Kobnithikulwong
3-9  Siriporn Kobnithikulwong
3-10 Siriporn Kobnithikulwong
3-11 Siriporn Kobnithikulwong
3-12 Siriporn Kobnithikulwong

## CHAPTER 4

4-1  Siriporn Kobnithikulwong
4-2  Siriporn Kobnithikulwong
4-3  Siriporn Kobnithikulwong
4-4  Siriporn Kobnithikulwong
4-5  Sargent Architectural Photography
4-6  Photo by George Cott/Taylor & Taylor Partnership
4-7  Siriporn Kobnithikulwong
4-8  Larry Wilson, Rink Design Partnership, Inc. © 2008 Joseph Lapeyra Photography
4-9  Larry Wilson © 2008 Joseph Lapeyra Photography
4-10 Larry Wilson © 2008 Joseph Lapeyra Photography

## CHAPTER 5

5-1  Siriporn Kobnithikulwong
5-2  Julia Sexton and Carly Jacobson
5-3  Siriporn Kobnithikulwong
5-4  Larry Wilson, Rink Design Partnership, Inc. © 2008 Joseph Lapeyra Photography
5-5  Larry Wilson, Rink Design Partnership, Inc. © 2008 Joseph Lapeyra Photography
5-6  Pavlik Design Team © 2008
5-7  Siriporn Kobnithikulwong
5-8  Amy Chen
5-9  Harmonic Runway by Christopher Janney/ Nick Merrick HEDRICH-BLESSING/AECOM Design
5-10 Photo by Brian Gassel/TVS
5-11 Designer HOK, Photography by Peter Cook, 2006

## CHAPTER 6

6-1  Siriporn Kobnithikulwong
6-2  Pavlik Design Team © 2008
6-3  Siriporn Kobnithikulwong
6-4  Craig Dugan@Hedrich Blessing
6-5  Designer HOK, Photography by Christopher Barrett of Hedrich Blessing, 2007
6-6  Designer HOK, Photography by Christopher Barrett of Hedrich Blessing, 2007
6-7  Designer HOK, Photography by Christopher Barrett of Hedrich Blessing, 2007
6-8  Nick Merrick HEDRICH-BLESSING/AECOM Design
6-9  Photo by Brian Gassel/TVS

## CHAPTER 7

7-1  Siriporn Kobnithikulwong
7-2  Pavlik Design Team © 2008
7-3  Pavlik Design Team © 2008
7-4  Pavlik Design Team © 2008
7-5  Pavlik Design Team © 2008
7-6  Photo by Phil Prowse/Flad Architects
7-7  Photo by Neil Rashba/Flad Architects

## CHAPTER 8

8-1  Siriporn Kobnithikulwong
8-2  Photo by Brian Gassel/TVS
8-3  Photo © Michael Moran

## CHAPTER 9

9-1  Siriporn Kobnithikulwong
9-2  Photo by Brian Gassel/TVS
9-3  Photo by Brian Gassel/TVS
9-4  Photo by Brian Gassel/TVS
9-5  Photo by Brian Gassel/TVS
9-6  Photo by Brian Gassel/TVS
9-7  Photo by Brian Gassel/TVS
9-8  Photo by Brian Gassel/TVS
9-9  Photo by Brian Gassel/TVS
9-10 Photo by Brian Gassel/TVS
9-11 Photo by Brian Gassel/TVS
9-12 Photo by Brian Gassel/TVS

# Index